Dream Porches and Sunrooms

Designing the Perfect Retreat

721·84
690

D

Dream Porches and Sunrooms

Designing the Perfect Retreat

Michael Snow

COLLINS|DESIGN

An Imprint of HarperCollinsPublishers

DREAM PORCHES AND SUNROOMS: DESIGNING THE PERFECT RETREAT

HarperCollins books may be purchased for educational, business, or sales promotion use.
For information, please write:
Special Markets Department, HarperCollins Publishers, 10 East 53rd Street, New York, NY 10022

First published in 2006 by:

Collins Design
An Imprint of HarperCollins*Publishers*
10 East 53rd Street
New York, NY 10022
Tel: (212) 207-7000
Fax: (212) 207-7654
collinsdesign@harpercollins.com
www.harpercollins.com

Distributed throughout the world by:
HarperCollins*Publishers*
10 East 53rd Street
New York, NY 10022
Fax: (212) 207-7654

Conceived and produced by Dolezal & Associates, Livermore, California

Library of Congress Cataloging in Publication Data
Snow, Michael, 1964-
    Dream porches and sunrooms : designing the perfect retreat / Michael
Snow.-- 1st ed.
        p. cm.
    ISBN 0-06-084728-X (hardcover)
1. Porches. 2. Sunspaces. 3. Architecture, Domestic. I. Title.
    NA3070.S66 2006
721'.84--dc22

                                        2005029200

ISBN-10:   0-06-084728-X
ISBN-13:   978-0-06-084728-9

Printed in China

Second Printing, 2006

3 5 7 9 8 6 4 2 Printing, 2006

The contributors and credits on pages 170-173 are hereby incorporated in the content of this page.

Contents

Introduction

When I worked as a waiter, before I became a design professional, I realized that my most discerning customers were those who also worked in the restaurant business. They knew about the food and its presentation, understood timing and order, and most of all appreciated excellent service. So I began serving all my tables as if every customer was an expert. It removed judgment and subjectivity from my job, and it allowed me to foster and maintain a professional attitude with every patron.

I approached this book the same way. Whether as a design expert or a home owner searching for ideas and direction, you'll appreciate the result of my efforts to communicate the features and impact of these porches in a satisfying and memorable way.

In this book, I show traditional wraparound porches mixed in with very contemporary designs. You'll see porches that are extensions of indoor living areas in their furnishings and finishes and others that are more or less enclosures of outdoor spaces. There are certainly those with enviable views of a natural setting (even if that's an intimate garden oasis in a busy urban neighborhood), while others are more introspective and self-contained, shielding a view or simply more attentive to activities within its borders.

Despite their obvious differences, every porch, veranda, and sunroom selected for this book is an example of great architecture—which I define as achieving a balance of form and function and a match between climate and convenience, resulting in a optimal living experience for each porch's owner.

I selected the porches, verandas, and sunrooms not just for their design excellence, but also to represent an extensive menu of ideas and distinct design details so each time you pick up this book you'll come away with new insight and inspiration for your porch. As was the case with my customers at the restaurants, I want you to come back to this book again and again, finding fresh ideas to consume with each repeat visit.

Porches are special places. You can have different experiences on the same porch, depending on whether you're there by yourself, part of a family gathering, or sharing a swing with a two-year-old child watching a first thunderstorm. It is also an intimate place that lets you experience nature in your own home.

Balancing this appeal, porches have a practical role in housing design, a contribution that has certainly changed as homes have modernized. Before air-conditioning, the out-

◄◄ A variety of basic materials, including concrete, wood, and metal, complement the dramatic design of this porch. In addition to effectively shielding views of neighboring yards on either side—thus focusing the view over a valley to a city skyline—the porch features a high ceiling to further enclose it and protect it from the elements—except a metal-clad circle cut out of the middle to trap the warmth of the sun and track its path across the floor. The effect is not only beautiful, but also practical, as capturing that warmth extends the usability of the porch throughout the day.

door climate in large part dictated the design of houses and porches. Porches were relied on for passive cooling and heating, to provide shade, and to create barriers to wind and rain. Simply, porches served primarily a functional purpose as shelters from the elements and transitional spaces between the outdoors and the inside of the house.

Today, thanks to indoor climate control, few homes are designed with a porch that helps manage the inside environment (though the emerging trend towards so-called "green" homes may mute that shift over time). For a time, the porch was considered unnecessary and in many cases was simply tacked on as a design element to appease consumer demand for what passed as traditional home design, an unfortunate trend that continues today.

But the porch has also experienced a revival as a vital component of a home's design, as it is one of the last places where designers can reflect the climate and prevailing site conditions as key elements in their craft. In addition to the weather of a particular area of the country, a designer must also consider the factors at play on a particular site, which may include microclimate, street noise, accessibility, views, and security.

Though often a neglected discipline, the consideration of such elements drives the design of a porch more than that of the house itself. After all, a house is all to often placed anywhere—a function of modern community planning—but a porch's placement must be a much more sensitive consideration of the conditions of the site, a subtle yet clear connection between the porch and nature.

Because porches have a less practical impact on modern homes today, they have shifted from being simply transitional spaces to integral ones on par with the rooms inside the house in their use, importance, and decor.

In today's homes, a porch has to be visible from inside the house, with multiple windows, wide doors, and similar (or the same) materials connecting the porch to the indoors, as you'll see in several of the projects and photographs in this book. They've become places where we go to relax, to simply watch, to talk, and to think. As we value those experiences, our porches evolve into dedicated areas that utilize the principles of interior design. Outdoor kitchens and dining areas, sleeping and reading nooks—in some cases, interior living is placed secondary to outdoor living spaces, as in the cabin-like screen-in porch pictured on pages 92–93. Another example is the dining porch seen on pages 104–105. There, the architect created an almost seamless transition from the kitchen to the porch, using similar forms, lighting, flooring material, and furniture that indicate an indoor space, but which are actually located outdoors.

The reverse is also true, as some porches are indoor extensions of the outdoor environment. On the screened porch on pages 122–123, for instance, a deck-like floor is carried to an outdoor staircase and open deck that connects the porch to the backyard, while the design of the porch takes maximum advantage of the view and environs.

I find that people often like a certain design, but can't quite understand why they like it. Their reaction is usually emotional or sensual, rather than practical or objective. Beyond the principles of scale, proportion, balance, ratio, and rhythm (all worthy and important objectives, if also difficult to articulate with an untrained eye), good—and certainly great—design is in the details.

For this book, I've selected porches, verandas, and sunrooms that showcase great architecture, construction, and details, and I've also chosen projects that point out how those features connect with each other to create a well-designed space. How a porch with an open rail (or no rail at all) is appropriate to maintain a view whether you're standing or sitting, while a solid railing offers privacy, blocks wind, and may even hide a view, perhaps creating ad-hoc seating—all, of course, in keeping with the overall architectural design of the house itself. Or, how a porch that's open on three sides facilitates cooling cross-breezes in a humid climate or vents smoke and smells from an outdoor kitchen, while an enclosed porch serves a more indoor function, as a sort of reception area for the main house.

Getting the details right is essential to every porch or sunroom no matter what the home's size or market value. As you'll see in this book, I have focused on modest as well as expensive or large-scale homes. Instead, I have paid attention to finding great porches and sunrooms, a good number of which happen to be attached to some very practical, down-to-earth homes—a great example being the beautiful, simple porch of the small Texas home shown on page 10.

It's the details that also connect the diverse architectural styles you'll see in this book. I felt it was critical to show porches and sunrooms from all parts of the country (and a

▲ This front porch on a Texas farmhouse is elegant in its simplicity, with an open design that creates the perception of a larger space. A reveal created by stopping the porch roof short of the sidewall allows just enough space for downspouts from the main roof above.

few in my native Canada) out of respect for the broad range of housing styles out there. I also wanted to provide you with as many ideas as possible as you consider your own home and the opportunity to create a porch or sunroom. Each picture is an occasion to focus on a special element—more than one, I hope—that inspires a greater appreciation for design and offers ideas you can apply in your own situation.

You'll find this book organized in a way that allows you to compare your own home or building site to the ones shown in the following pages. The first two chapters introduce the porch and sunroom, giving glimpses of the differences to be found in porches that result from new construction, remodeling, or addition. The next three chapters rifle in to show design examples where porches enhance the value, aesthetics, and appeal of homes of varied architecture. A chapter discusses the outfitting of a porch with furnishings, fittings, appointments, and other details. Finally, the book concludes with a practical review of basic construction knowledge, revealing the steps your design team and builder will execute to build you a porch. As an aid to help you find a qualified designer, there's also a detailed resource list that provides information about the designers who contributed their projects to the book.

I tried to think about how people would use this book. I considered every reader a prospective or current porch user—if not an architectural design expert—who wants to embellish his or her personal experience when designing or improving a porch. This book will enlighten you with practical examples of the many features that make a porch into the kind of environment that we all seem to value. It's an awareness that will serve you well, regardless of your level of design experience or your skills for communicating the elements of a good design to others. This book is a tool for achieving good design, encouraging and enabling you to come away with great ideas every time you visit it.

Michael Snow

▲ A small screened porch fronting a guest house behind the main residence offers a protected and private entrance. The stone path, simple structural columns, and low-pitched metal roof echo details of the main house.

Wide Open Places

Porches come in all shapes and sizes, and they serve nearly every purpose any home owner could imagine. Consider the comforting symmetry and generous depth of a wraparound front porch, the intimacy of a backyard screened porch, the warmth and spacious atmosphere of a sunroom, and the drama of a veranda that serves as a dual purpose outdoor entertainment center for a swimming pool and garden. No matter where they are or how they function, great porches welcome you, inspire you to stay, allow you to relax, and permit you to enjoy the scenery framed by their openings, railings, and rooflines.

The best porch, veranda, or sunroom complements and enhances the design of the main house so that the entire structure is cohesive in its finishing touches and form. A consistent palette of colors, textures, angles, and fixtures combines to achieve a comfortable, well-scaled setting, a place you long to be. Sometimes a simple, thoughtful twist in the form of a whimsical sconce or pendant light, an intriguing floor finish, or an eclectic mix of furnishings adds personality.

Great porches also purposefully extend indoor living space, providing enough area for furniture and potted plants without impeding on traffic patterns and opening to views and outdoor areas beyond. Ideally, a porch, veranda, or sunroom is accessible from several rooms or areas of the house, enabling you to step out on a whim or open up the entire space to accommodate party guests.

Perhaps what porches do best is combine the security and shelter of the indoors with the true feeling of being out-of-doors. Under its protective shelter, a porch provides a full view of a mountain lake or the sight of an oncoming thunderstorm backlit by the sun, the sound of the breeze rustling through the leaves of an oak tree or across a field of tall meadow grass rippling like ocean waves, and the scents of a recent rainstorm, or ripening grapes on the vine during harvest season, or heavenly aromas emanating from roses wafting up from a border planting beside its railing.

Simply put, porches allow you to experience the natural world while also protecting you from it. Porches offer a soothing respite, a retreat—though still within sight of your family and the activities of daily life. Done well, a porch is a gift that delivers something new almost every time you open a door to enjoy it, unwrapping a different scene of colors, sounds, and scents.

◄◄ A variety of design elements combine on this second-story porch to deliver dramatic views of California's wine country while providing a comfortable outdoor retreat for family and friends. The high beamed ceiling and arched openings, a staple of Colonial Spanish architecture, frame the view and allow cross-breezes through the porch; a thin iron railing allows those seated to still enjoy the vista. The depth and length of the porch allow for several conversation areas without blocking foot traffic, while multiple sets of doors from the house extend the living space outdoors.

▼ This porch addition uses architectural elements and finishes of the house to achieve a cohesive look. It also gains distinction with unique features, such as a rounded gable window.

▲ Spun from the corner of a contemporary house, this screened porch offers protection from pests and a place for contemplation overlooking a garden and koi pond. Its minimalist construction employs clear fir columns and a slatted ceiling illuminated by a single fan-and-light unit and accent fixtures on the columns.

▲ The semi-circular design of this porch creates a deep bump-out into the surrounding landscape. Only a step up from grade, it requires no railing and grants easy access to the yard. Paired columns and a thin-plank ceiling complement the home's style.

PERFECT PORCHES

What makes an ideal porch? Perhaps it's the amount of space it offers for furniture and entertaining. Maybe it's how the porch frames a spectacular view. What about the look and feel of its materials and finishes, or their ability to withstand the outdoor elements? Of course, a great porch is integral to the overall design of the house—whatever style it may be—enriching it as a logical extension and architectural feature. It maintains a comfortable, human scale to avoid feeling cavernous or impersonal. It delivers interesting details and textures that change as natural and artificial light passes across, creating shadow lines of relief and revealing new colors, hues, and tones. Ultimately, though, what determines a perfect porch is whether it improves the quality of life for the people using it, creating a special, treasured place like no other they experience.

▲ This all-glass glazed, aluminum-framed sun-room suits the sea-facing site of this modern, contemporary-style home. The stark yet inviting geometry of the window framing complements its clean, sharp lines while providing an appropriate contrast to the white stucco finish that is evocative of the Greek or Spanish Mediterranean.

▶ This "garden room" connects the house to nature, with views to a sloping hillside. The floor-to-ceiling windows are divided at the same height as the railing along the front of the porch, providing a consistent element between the stone foundation and the beaded ceiling and blurring the distinction between inside and out.

Like the personal preferences the owners share, a porch reflects and accentuates the style elements of its adjacent house. In that sense, every well-designed porch becomes unique, regardless of its owners' individual taste in architecture. A radiused porch on a Queen Anne Victorian-style home overlooking a pine-rimmed lake, a three-season sunroom of a suburban ranch house on the prairie, and a sleeping loft extended from a mountain cabin with its view of glacial cirques and horns can be judged with equal merit. Always appropriate to its site and situation, each porch stands on its own; it is a perfect element suited to its circumstances, climates, architecture, views, and, most important, its owners' tastes and lifestyle.

◀◀ The ceiling of this deep-set porch adds signature interest and intricacy to a beaded-plank finish. Following the curved line of the porch roof, the deep profile created by the trim moulding creates a coffered ceiling that adds depth, detail, and shadow lines.

◀ Set over a rear-opening garage, this porch provides several points of access, and it follows the symmetry and materials of the house and patio. Notice how the main entry to the house—on the left end of the porch—is set back and steps up, allowing the door to swing open without intruding on the main traffic area.

Porches are for more than just sitting; in fact, they serve several functions, both obvious and subtle, practical yet whimsical. In pleasant climates and if properly protected from the elements, porches serve as outdoor dining areas, perhaps with a full kitchen setup, to entertain friends and family. On the front of a house, a porch welcomes guests. When facing an undisturbed or undeveloped landscape, porches encourage personal reflection.

Porches are a transition to the outdoors, allowing you to decide whether to step out farther, or retreat to the house. Potted plants and window boxes blur the lines still further, bringing nature onto the porch itself.

Porches also lead you on a path of discovery, offering a clear direction to an outdoor feature, such as a swimming pool or garden. With furniture, they beg you to sit and chat or read a book, laugh on the swing, or wait for the mail. They point the way, but also entice you to take your time getting there.

▲ This porch, set atop a third-story tower, delivers a spectacular panoramic view. Large enough for ample furnishings and potted plants, it features a ceiling fan to supplement natural cross-breezes. A wrought-iron rail provides safety without blocking the view. Wood beams over the openings suit the Mediterranean style of the house.

▲ A total commitment to symmetry, from the window design to the matching furniture placement, makes for an inviting front porch; slightly raising it above grade also provides a sense of privacy. A curved beam adds space and reduces the volume out of the tall, open-ceilinged portico (with a pitch that matches the two dormers) and helps frame a suspended leaded-glass window.

▶▶ A high ceiling, slender columns, an open railing, and the use of a light trim color create a relaxing airiness. The spacious portico helps identify the front door while providing a distinctive feature whether seen it's from the curb or on the porch.

Time was that your front door was the way family and guests entered your home, and the importance of a welcoming front porch was paramount. But in many cases, today's homes have three-car garages with doors leading directly into the house, which relegate the "main entry" to second-class status. It doesn't have to be so. While your front door and porch may not necessarily be the most-used entrance of the house, they are still your home's first and best opportunity to impress guests and passers-by. Done well, your front porch will catch the eye and inspire the imagination; strangers and guests will wonder what it's like to sit on those comfortable chairs with a refreshing beverage or enjoy the relaxing motion of the bench swing, and they will envy the detailing and sense of history that your porch inspires and preserves.

Front porches come in many scales and plans, from those at-grade and nearly public spaces to others perched high above the street that create a more private retreat. A solid railing, deep roof overhang, and fascia treatment create a sense of shelter, while an open rail and high ceiling make possible views in and out of the porch. The approach to a porch is also telling: a wide staircase and a straight path encourage visitors, while a meandering walk to a switch-back set of stairs elicits a sense of mystery, wonder, and anticipation. Of course, every well-designed porch is also in harmony with its surroundings, a complement to the house and grounds; it delivers the complete package.

Positively Porch

You may have a vision of enjoying a porch, veranda, or sunroom, but you need to know how to make that dream a reality. Your best starting place is to concentrate on what you want. Do you want a place to gather with family and friends, or would you rather have a quiet spot from which to watch birds and other wildlife? A well-designed porch adds value to your home; getting there requires careful planning and setting realistic expectations.

From start to finish, you'll have decisions to make. The first, and most important, is deciding why you want to add or remodel a porch. There are many right answers; the right porch for you is one that best suits your lifestyle, whether it's simply a place to relax in the evening, a space to entertain, an outdoor kitchen or dining area, a way to connect with your neighbors, an opportunity to capture a view, or a way to improve your home's curb appeal. Besides providing an outdoor retreat, porches add significant amounts of multifunctional living space. They are often more economical (and less intrusive) than a room addition or an interior remodeling project, yet offer similar features and the same amount of space. So dedicate thought to deciding your purpose, articulate and discuss it, and prioritize your requirements and wishes to fuel the design and construction of your porch project.

There are other considerations, too. You'll want to establish a budget, select a designer and contractor, and choose the materials, fixtures, systems, and finishes that will go into your porch. Remember that local covenants, conditions, and restrictions (CC&Rs), building codes, and other municipal regulations have a say in the design and construction of your porch. All of these elements are important, and you'll balance them to develop the best design solution, plans, and approaches to the building phase.

It's prudent to take these steps one at a time. Place your project in the knowledgeable hands of a design professional and a qualified contractor early on. Together, they'll make sure each decision is thoughtful and unrushed and every base is covered. With the designer and builder, you'll match the porch or sunroom to your house's style, location, and site conditions. You'll avoid making obvious mistakes or achieving poor results due to haste or thoughtless execution. Trust your designer and contractor to translate your vision of a porch or sunroom to a finished project that suits your house, complies with codes, and delivers lasting value.

◄◄ Dedicated outdoor cooking and dining areas are an increasingly popular and feature-rich aspect of new porches. Tucked neatly into a corner—as a formal dining room might be inside the house—the space is unaffected by foot traffic and other nearby activity; massive materials and intense colors, a low arched opening to the outside, and a dark, open-beam ceiling protect its sense of intimacy. Many of its features accommodate its use—a high ceiling, a nearby opening, and a pendant fan that help exhaust smoke from the barbecue—while also imparting the comfort and security intrinsic to a rustic farmhouse.

▲ A sloping lot suits a porch that is set high off of grade, placing your sight line above or into the foliage of surrounding trees instead of offering a view of their trunks or roots. The effect, especially with screened window openings, is akin to a treehouse—and such porches are perfect settings for sleeping on warm summer evenings as well as places to simply relax under a cool canopy of trees.

BY THE BOOK

Regardless of its intended use, the actual design and placement of a porch, veranda, or sunroom is often dictated by the practical matters of the orientation of the house and its location and setting. The lot may slope away or into the house, for instance, or a code or building regulation might govern the height of the porch, its distance from the sidewalk or property line, or even its scale, proportions, and finishes.

Another critical site consideration is climate, from the direction of its prevailing winds and falling rain to dealing with falling leaves and flying insects. The microclimate of a porch location also includes its proximity to nearby structures and the street; consider not only the sites views—which may be either intrusive or attractive—but also the issues of noise and security. Even a porch that is designed to encourage a bond with neighbors needs to be shielded to guarantee your privacy and protect your property. All of these considerations are at play in porch design, driving the scale, dimension, and finishes of its every component.

◀ Porches often serve to temper and soften the mass of a strong or dominant feature or color and reduce a potentially intimidating facade to a more comfortable and inviting, human scale.

▼ Newly developed communities with narrow lots and little space between surrounding homes mean opportunities for rear-facing porches overlooking their backyards. Such porches both serve as covered decks and maintain privacy from the street and sides.

In addition to climate and microclimate considerations, a porch, sunroom, or veranda must also suit the style of the house. Porches integrate issues of proper proportion, scale, complementary materials, consistency among design elements, and detailing.

Notice in the photograph on the right, for instance, the use of split-beam columns on the upper and lower porches. They make the design consistent on both levels of the home, and they are proportional in scale to their respective porches; the stone used at the base of each lower column is a theme that carries throughout the dwelling as well.

Contrast those split-beam columns with those of the house pictured above. Here, the columns are evenly spaced along the length of the porch—save the last one, which has been cleverly removed to allow a full and more inviting view of the front door.

The varied treatments of columns in these two examples reveal the depth of consideration that your professional designer brings to your porch's detail work. As he or she works with you to plan your porch's appearance, keep these issues in mind, since the new or remodeled porch should embrace the overall design of your house and enhance all of its elements, rather than detract from your home.

Access to your porch should be both apparent and safe to anyone approaching it, regardless of the design and placement of your steps or path. How you provide or restrict access says much about the porch's functionality and how it will be perceived. On a front entry porch, for instance, a wide staircase centered on the front door invites people to visit; perhaps you might top it with a gabled or arched roof overhang and flank its front elevation with an open-railing design. A porch set at or just above grade—level with the ground—outfitted with an open set of steps along its entire length is also akin to a public invitation; such designs permit visitors to enter and exit the porch from any point. Either public porch extends the use of the porch or veranda beyond its cover, providing places for people to sit and engage in conversation or contemplation.

A staircase that enters from the side and weaves its way to the porch, meanwhile, conveys your intent for a more private space and suggests that it is reserved for your personal use. Achieve the same effect by using a pathway leading to a single set of steps; a hedgerow or half wall that limits the view of the rest of the porch amplifies your message.

Any desire you might have to dictate access to your porch is subject to the existing conditions of your site, your home's design, and the applicable building codes or other municipal regulations. In addition, the details of the steps, stairs, or at-grade path leading to the porch must be consistent with the porch and the house. If the porch features a solid railing and matches the exterior siding material of the house, so should the design of the handrail flanking the stairs.

◄ Maintaining accurate proportion is a key consideration for an effective front porch, helping draw the eye to the front door. Notice how the use of split columns replicates the sidelites on either side of the entry door, while the beam spanning the opening mirrors the mid-span trim over the door. Even the walkway design narrows as you approach the entry, drawing you in.

In addition to steps and staircases, the presence or absence of a porch's railing and its form also is an important design element. Beyond simply providing an opening to indicate a point of entry onto the porch, the railing sets the tone for the overall structure.

A porch without a railing, for instance, presents a very public face. It encourages traffic to flow unimpeded and grants a near-seamless connection with the open landscape beyond the porch's roof. In accordance with most building codes, open porches are only allowed for structures either set at or within a single step above grade. The absence of a railing lets the floor, ceiling, and vertical columns of a porch fully frame a landscape view.

If you desire, shrubs and other landscape designs act as "soft" railings, enabling you to direct access to the porch without building a permanent barrier. Often, porches without railings are more contemporary in design approach and may not suit the style of a traditional house, such as an Arts and Crafts or Victorian style. More traditional homes require railings to enclose and finish their porches and maintain their overall character.

For porches more than a step above grade—and those where wind protection is a requirement of their sites—rails of some kind are required to provide safety barriers and protection. Open railing designs allow views onto and out of the entire porch, while solid half walls block marginal views and instill higher levels of privacy; for a step between the two, choose semi-solid railings with wide stiles and narrow spaces.

Whether open or solid, wood or wrought iron, your choice of railing is a matter of personal taste balanced with issues of practical safety and privacy concerns.

Easy Access Checklist

Follow these useful and code-compliant guidelines to create safe access to your porch:

✓ A minimum headroom of 6 feet 8 inches between the top step and the ceiling.

✓ Stair risers between 4 inches and 8 inches high; treads no less than 9 inches wide.

✓ Railings at least 36 inches tall, with stiles spaced no more than 4 inches apart.

✓ Handrails on stairs with four or more risers, located between 34 and 38 inches above the tread.

✓ Landings up to 36 inches wide must be at least the width of the stair (can be wider).

On-grade porches afford more flexibility in materials and design, allowing you to control points of access with a railing and extend paving materials into the porch floor.

Porches and sunrooms are all about making connections—with people, with nature, with outdoor features, and with the indoor environment. You and your design and construction team will determine the linkages you'll make, and how.

Your house and lot will influence those connections. If your house sits on a hillside or your porch is off of the second story, for instance, it likely will be raised above grade and will feel connected more to the house than to people passing by below. Just the opposite is true on a level parcel, where your activities on the porch are much more public and your connections with your surroundings are more immediate.

Site considerations also determine how your porch interacts with your house. A porch shielded from the public may have access at several points into various rooms, while a more public porch might have just a single point of entry—at the front door—and then wrap around the home.

Your porch's interplay with nature and the outdoor features of your home, such as a pool or garden, is another consideration for added function. In addition to allowing easy access to those features from the porch, think about how to view them from inside the house and through the porch, perhaps enhancing the transition by using the same floor or decking material in both locations. Thoughtful placement of glass windows and doors and the design of your porch's structural columns and its railings can enhance a porch's connection with the outdoors.

Lastly, maximize your porch's potential to connect you to other people, either neighbors or guests. Whether your porch is set high off grade or level with the street, attention to design details can make it as inviting as you wish. At times, you might prefer to stand on it alone, looking down to the street's walkways; on other occasions, you would welcome the chance to attract a visitor with the golden glow of your porch's overhead lamps.

▲ Subtle differences of slope extend the metal-clad roof of this home over its porches. The shal-lower slope of the lower sections still permits full head heights for the porches beneath them.

THINKING ABOUT DETAILS

Simply, details make the difference between a ho-hum porch and one that is cherished and envied. But it's a myth that your porch details must always and exactly match those of your house; it's more appropriate to complement your home's features, keeping the details in character and designing with respect for what's in place.

Often, the truly important details are very subtle. While a porch's structural columns and railing might complement—or even replicate—the form and finish of the siding and window trim of the house, look closer and you may see a simple band of color within the ceiling trim that picks up the natural stain of the deck boards below, or a tile pattern in the floor that flows through the entry arch and onto an adjacent patio. The lines of the fascia may align perfectly along the length of the porch, or the pitch of the porch roof is the same as that of the main house. A similar, if subtly different, grid pattern might fill the space between the railing and the windows to achieve better scale and proportion.

Details are much more than matching materials. They reveal themselves in subtle differences in form and proportion, color and contrast, and in other ways barely noticeable.

▲ A front porch, perfectly proportioned and detailed to the design of the house, adds dimension and depth to the home's facade and presents a welcoming approach to visitors.

▲ While appropriate to the home's original design, this flat and simple elevation offers no weather protection and lacks dimension. The front door nearly disappears into the facade. It is blocked by shrubs and is hard to reach.

UNDERSTANDING THE PROCESS

While your design professional and contractor should guide you through the entire process of creating or enhancing your porch or sunroom, it benefits you to gain a basic understanding of how they each approach design and building it so you can make thoughtful decisions and contend with any of the inevitable hiccups to planning or scheduling along the way.

It's a good idea to work out with your design-build team in advance a complete schedule that outlines the progress of the project, including time for getting your plans approved by the local authority and obtaining the periodic building inspections required for code compliance. In addition, resolve how you will request and they will accommodate changes, so that everyone is clear about the impact of ad-hoc alterations on the budget and schedule.

Communication is critical to any successful project. Feel comfortable from the outset in asking questions and receiving meaningful answers. Meet regularly with your designer and contractor to discuss their progress, problems, and next steps. An educated client who respects the design and construction process is perhaps the greatest asset to any project.

Water Views

Scenic views of a sandy or rocky shore, a tumbling river, or a placid lake inspire and influence the design and placement of a porch, along with the materials used for its construction. Whether perched on a lofty height or found low and close to the shore, the proximity of water means moisture and wind, two factors that weigh heavily in every architect's, builder's, or designer's mind as the plan for the porch is realized. At its heart, orienting your porch to capture an optimal view may mean some carefully considered compromises.

Think about how you'll place sheltering walls on the porch to deflect chilly winds off the water while maintaining an unobstructed landscape, or replace them with transparent, glazed openings or shutters. As another alternative, install a convertible porch that can be left wide open during a season of warm breezes or become completely enclosed in stormy times of the year. Plantings of trees, shrubs, and native grasses serve both aesthetic and practical purposes in such settings; they partially block or redirect winds to provide shelter, and they channel drifting sand away from pathways, stairs, and entry doors.

Seal natural wooden surfaces with breathable varnishes or epoxy-based coatings to protect them from near-constant mist and condensation, or paint them with mold-resistant finishes. Apply composite synthetic floorings, finish floor surfaces with masonry, or use naturally moisture-resistant woods such as cedar, teak, ipe, and other dense tropicals for an easy-to-maintain porch.

A porch in a site near a river or creek also means special design considerations are required. Such sites are frequently shaded by surrounding ridges or tall trees, so include provisions for ample natural and artificial light on the porch, and plan for falling leaves or needles when you choose the roofing material and gutters of the structure. A home-site near a seasonal stream that is subject to periods of high water may call for a raised perimeter or pier foundation for your porch; it could even require you to install a break-water or flood channel to mitigate flooding and protect your home.

For any water-view home with a porch, the balance of these and other practical considerations with aesthetic placement means choices and trade-offs. The projects found on the following pages show that careful designs made it possible to integrate each of them with its unique waterside setting. For every site built, there was one or more other possible solutions; each masterfully demonstrates a design paired with its locale.

◄◄ A curved covered porch overlooking the Pacific Ocean from a cliffside home near Vancouver, British Columbia, serves as an intimate dining area—though guests are sure to linger here long after dessert. The wood columns, railing, and ceiling treatment, as well as the furniture and stone floor, complement the soothing effect of the spectacular view. Dimmer-controlled, low-voltage recessed lights draw attention to the elegant columns as evening falls over the scene.

▲ Bridging the space between the main house and a guest retreat, this covered porch creates a communal area offering ready access to the open terrace and water beyond. Cedar shingles, sandblasted structural fir beams and trim, and a copper-colored roof finish complement the natural colors of a huge boulder native to the two-acre site that was dynamited in two to allow for the steps that lead to the house.

As visitors approach, the porch frames a stunning view of British Columbia's Strait of Georgia. Its open design allows ocean breezes to pass through; along with steel ties to the massive rock outcropping, the breezeway relieves lateral pressure on the twin, all-glass living wings from strong gales, locally called squamish winds.

◀ The site's northern exposure and spectacular water view was the perfect setting for the home's two-winged design, a concept mimicked by the cleaved rock outcropping and effectively integrated by the center porch and natural materials. Minimal views and connections into the porch from either living space contrast the vast amount of glass used on their respective facades. A lack of artificial light on the porch encourages the use of more intimate alternatives, such as the candles on the outdoor dining table.

▲ The owners of this refurbished lakeside cabin enjoy expansive views of the water from their generous rear porch, a vista that can also be seen from the inside through several floor-to-ceiling windows. The ceiling fans help move air in the home's humid southern climate, supplementing natural breezes that are encouraged through the porch's open design. The vertical strips added to the columns on the right side of the porch conceal a system of metal tracks and splines that enable the owners to attach temporary screens to enclose that end of the space.

▲ The absence of a rail across the front of this porch allows a full view from inside the house to the back yard and the lake beyond, through full-height windows featuring energy-efficient dual-pane glass and vinyl frame construction. Tough but comfortable wicker furniture withstands the elements while enhancing the porch's simple elegance and design.

▶ Classic looks combine with modern technology: The divided lites of the windows complement the home's architectural style. This unit's double-mulled construction—a style in which a single installed unit appears to be two windows—reduces labor costs.

▼ Instead of a railing, shrubs and natural vegetation will eventually block access to the front of the porch without intruding on the lake view while also directing people to use the steps on the left end of the porch.

With the lake and boat launch acting as a secondary approach to the house, the porch is the home's first impression to many visitors, making it as equally important as the front of the house. The gentle, grassy slope invites family and friends to enjoy the porch and its lakeside location.

▼ A sand-colored concrete floor and all-glass sliding doors blur the transition from the indoors, while wind-sheltered outdoor living spaces offer comfort and dramatic ocean views.

▲Wind-sheltered wings enable the owners to relax and enjoy their ocean oasis.

▲ Decking made from recycled polymers stands up to the coastal climate and sea air, weathering to a soothing gray. Broad steps unfold to the beach, providing an extra place to sit and relax for casual conversation while helping to break up the home's mass.

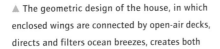 The geometric design of the house, in which enclosed wings are connected by open-air decks, directs and filters ocean breezes, creates both glimpses and full views of the water, shelters outdoor living spaces, and casts dramatic shadows across the vertical cedar siding.

▲ Adhering to coastal building codes for both seismic and flood conditions, the home features foundation walls that deflect waves and shield the structure, but that also break away in the event of a tsunami, allowing water to flow under the house.

A deep overhang helps define the porch, traps cool air, and provides maximum protection from the desert sun. The slatted wraparound railing—set on a short concrete wall that somewhat shields the outdoor soaking tub—allows ample air flow through the space.

▶A private retreat is situated off the master suite on the second floor, and the covered balcony overlooks the open-air terrace below.

◀◀ A serene, man-made lake weaves through the home's desert neighborhood.

▲ Copper on the underside of the roof, railings, and fascia reflects light and the occasional water ripple off the lake below, creating interesting light play from daybreak to long past sunset.

◀ The railing design serves as a transition between the mass of the home's washed concrete brick walls and the open sky. Clad over wide-set vertical steel posts and then welded horizontally between them, the fixed copper rails (as well as other copper features used on the home's exterior) will weather to a natural patina that enhances the contemporary design of the house and its concrete facade.

▶▶ Mosaic tiles on the floor and rising up the sides and onto the tub's lip are carried outside from the master bathroom. Combined with the glass-enclosed shower and matching tub on the opposite side of the glass, the tiny tiles in different hues of a single base color reinforce the definition of space and unite the outdoor extension of a luxurious bath while adding a different texture and feel compared to a traditional porch floor.

◄◄ Sunrooms maximize views (even those of the ocean shrouded in fog) and create a more direct connection with the outdoors. Notice how the door is set at the same angle as the floor tiles, a diagonal design carried out to the patio.

▲ The views from this room are vastly different on a foggy day than on one with clear skies, setting a varied mood in the same space. The cool ocean climate keeps heat gain through the glass to a comfortable minimum.

▲ Unlike a traditional porch, a sunroom is usually completely enclosed with glass walls. As a consequence, it requires careful consideration of complementary materials, forms, proportions, and scale, and must allow for venting of excess heat.

▶ A pair of covered porches overlooking Lake Washington near Seattle offer the privacy, view, and appealing environment enjoyed by all great retreats, providing shelter while capturing scenes of the landscaped garden and water beyond.

▼ A series of French doors and matching fixed windows connect the interior of the house to the porch and lake view, effectively emphasizing the home's connection with nature. In a very real sense, the walkway and dock area are extensions of the house and its porch.

▲ An open-air center deck connects a quiet sitting area off the master suite (top background) to a covered outdoor kitchen (opposite page). The architect combined copper railings with a tropical hardwood to create rich and durable finishes. The two-toned railing system exemplifies the principles of a Craftsman-style bungalow.

▶ A totem pole pays tribute to the colorful history of the surrounding area's native culture.

▲ Montana ledgestone, accented with sandstone on the fireplace that serves the outdoor kitchen and dining area, is a unifying element, continuing on the home's main chimney. This stone pattern repeats on the landscape wall (top, opposite page). A high, open ceiling aids ventilation, while the sitting area across the way features a lower, beadboard ceiling for a more intimate feel.

◄ The space under the open, peaked ceiling created by the overhanging gable roof, featuring the notches and bolts of log home construction, is served by a single overhead lamp that supplements light coming through the windows or provides comforting night light late in the evening.

◄ The intricate construction of the log-framed, open gable end, set midway within the overhanging roof, frames the windows behind it and creates a human scale for the porch below. The gable's horizontal beam draws the eye down to the porch, directing it to the attention of visitors and providing it with a visual enclosure. The wide steps are suitable for seating, while native boulders shield the open underside of the porch from view and add a distinctive design element.

◄◄ The long pier on the lake aligns with the stairs and front door, guiding guests to the 46-foot-long, 14-foot-deep wraparound porch. This elevation, in fact, was designed as the front of the house, and opens through three sets of doors into an open living area, enabling occasional gatherings to spill outside onto the porch.

▲ A porch swing is the perfect perch from which to enjoy a parade of wildlife throughout the day, from mallards, pelicans, and swans in the morning to deer, raccoons, and the occasional opossum in the evening, not to mention river otters frolicking in the lake beyond. The freestanding design of the rustic swing made of peeled spruce permits the owners to move it out of the way for a party or place it in new positions to capture different views from the porch. The swing's climate-tough construction is a close match to the porch's materials.

◄ Accents make the difference, whether it be a whimsical dinner bell (top) or a steel post that holds the logs off the porch deck to mitigate standing water around the wood post (left). Among a plethora of wildlife, squirrels have become so comfortable on the porch that they jump up on the owners' lap for food while they enjoy a spectacular and unobstructed view of Mt. Shasta, a dormant volcano.

►► The understated front door of the house acts more like a window, framing the view of the mountain from the inside and allowing natural light into the house. The use of a contrasting trim color sets apart the windows and doors from the logs, creating clean lines and making them easily identifiable.

▲ The porch's slate tile floor matches that of the pool deck, tying the two areas together. Similarly, the furniture complements the iron railing, which allows a clear view of the pool area and the ocean beyond.

▲ While a solid, beadboard-finished ceiling protects most of the second-story porch, a glazed trellised cutout adds natural light to the space and the home's interior. Located near Vancouver, B.C., on a site overlooking the Pacific Ocean, the porch gets its share of weather; hence, the glass-paneled cut-out shields the outdoor dining area, allowing rainwater to run down the roof's slope to a gutter on the fascia. It gives the owners maximum flexibility of use for the porch. Notice, too, how the trellis beams are doubled up, mimicking the columns.

▲ The heaviness of the lower terrace anchors the lighter treatment of the porch above, including an iron railing that almost disappears against the slate-finished shingle siding and generous windows. Horizontal lines scored into the concrete of the lower level help break up its mass.

◀◀ One of the architect's personal favorites among many outdoor spaces around the house, this quiet spot in the corner of the porch captures the calming feel of the house, offering a place to relax. Set just a step above grade, the porch maintains a close connection with the landscape— a bond reinforced by the historically accurate columns that frame full views of the garden and Nantucket Sound. Among several subtle details, the floor planks end at a diagonal stop, creating a cleaner edge and serving as a visual transition as the side porch turns the corner to the front of the house.

▲ Set on a hill, the house is designed and sited to hug the ground, even as the land slopes away from the entry. As you approach, the house presents a narrow elevation and a deep, welcoming porch with a low-sloped roof that combine to create a comfortable, human scale that indicates a cozy cottage. Even a glimpse of the wraparound porch isn't enough to give away its full depth and extensive views of the water along one side, preserving that drama for when you enter the house.

▼ A dining pergola, nestled on the more private side of the house, features a trellised roof and French doors that provide direct access to the indoor living areas. An adjacent porch offers intimate shelter from native winds and wraps around the back of the house to connect with the oceanside elevation.

► The elevation opposite from the sea side provides additional outdoor spaces shielded from prevailing winds and offers an intimate garden in contrast to the vastness of the ocean view. Native shrubs separate the spaces, allowing each of them to maintain their individuality.

▲ The oceanside elevation maximizes the home's hilltop location, with a long, deep porch extending along its public rooms. The spacing of the columns signals points of entry; without railings between them, they encourage use of the entire porch at any point. Granite slabs align with the French doors to serve as helpful steps and further connect the house with the surrounding landscape. An enclosed breezeway, which separates the main house from a guest suite, features an open deck and a covered porch that wraps around the back of the house to join one on the opposite side. Notice how the fascia is in strict alignment across the entire elevation of the structure—another subtle yet critical detail found in this well-designed house.

▶ Double, full-height French doors opening out to the porch make the interior spaces feel larger and further its connections to the outside, as do the exterior elements, such as the column shape and detailing, ceiling color, and rustic flooring. A slightly higher ceiling inside also helps the space appear larger, a modern twist on traditionally small saltbox rooms.

The Architect Speaks

Nantucket has a strict historic district commission governing the design of every building on the island. To comply with the commission's guidelines, we used basic historic forms and details, such as shingle siding, painted white trim, divided-lite windows, and square columns.

With a house on a hill, it was necessary to maintain a human scale. Porch areas, kept nearly at grade to make them almost part of the landscape, help ground the house and minimize its height and grandness. I design porches to frame views and reduce glare into the house, appropriate steps for a house overlooking Nantucket Sound.

Wind is a constant issue in this climate. Several spaces along the home's exterior give the owners space to enjoy the outdoors in varied weather and for different social events—a solution they requested but could not visualize. The surrounding porches and decks open up to the kitchen, dining room, living room, and a guest suite. French doors expand the passages to the outdoors, making the openings and rooms feel larger.

This house is somewhat unusual. A guest suite completes the lower level. The next floor is a master suite, and a separate guest house provides four more bedrooms. The main house replaced an existing residence, which was relocated elsewhere on the island. We take pride in designing homes for and with our clients, a philosophy that is both challenging and requires constant experimentation with architectural forms.

—William Martin McGuire, AIA, principal

▲ An open deck provides a bit of visual relief from the covered porch areas while also allowing visitors to enjoy an occasional clear, calm day. Though quite a different experience from the other outdoor spaces, the deck also affords more space for party goers to spill over from the covered areas without becoming disconnected from the house. The two-story guest suite maintains its connection to the main house, yet is obviously separated by the change in the roof height of the enclosed breezeway and the exclusive use of a bay window on its elevation.

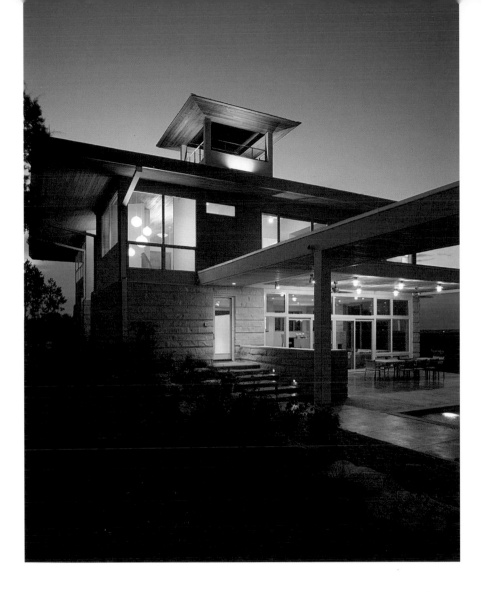

▲ The main house features a third-level tower porch lookout with a panoramic view that harkens back to widows' walks seen atop period homes of the region. A floating beam encloses the back of the pool area and shelters a breezeway to the guest house.

◄◄ A second floating beam across the front of the pool frames a dramatic view of Lake Travis, near Austin, while also stabilizing the trellised roof of the porch and creating a sense of enclosure for the pool. The "window" formed by the beam mimics a picture window of the same view from the inside of the house. The fountain is reminiscent of old-time courtyards, with its cooling waters and splashing sounds.

▶ Simple light fixtures illuminate the outdoor dining area on the trellised porch, while a ceiling fan helps cool the space in the heat of the day. A pair of center-opening glass patio doors and a low threshold create a graceful transition to the porch. The pool and fountain beyond extend the sights and sounds of the lake to interior spaces. The trellis slats, made of low-maintenance aluminum, filter light while allowing ventilation.

◀◀ Reflecting elements of the house, garden, and water views, this two-level porch provides plenty of entertainment spaces and opportunities to enjoy the outdoors while also maintaining a close connection to the home's interior.

▲ The entire porch is segmented. Each section serves an interior space, shields its area from the ocean climate, and has varied column, roof, and ceiling treatments. The depth of the porches helps control the amount of sunlight and heat from the south-facing elevation.

▲ Skylights bring a measure of daylight into the deep upper porch, supplementing a pendant ceiling fixture and fireplace sconces for a comfortable conversation and generous entertainment area. Instead of glass panels, a steel railing still enables through-views while also blending into the trees. Unlike glass, the railing won't reflect light, fog up, form condensation, or otherwise create an unintended barrier to the dramatic ocean view. It's also more appropriate to the style of the house.

▲ A wide, sliding, all-glass door frames a full view from the house through the porch to the water while also creating an ample opening for guests to flow easily between the two spaces.

▶ A gentle piano-like curve delivers a dramatic, interesting elevation. Light colored finishes on the major structural elements and most exposed materials, including the concrete steps, mitigate any sense of feeling closed in, as do the steps running the length of the porch.

▲ Aspects of the landscape design and the home's architecture meet in the porches, from the concrete tops and stone bases of the plant pedestals that are repeated on the floor and the fireplace, to the beadboard and coffered ceiling treatment akin to those inside the house.

The Architect Speaks

We were faced with several objectives in designing this house. The owners are all about entertaining and wanted a house that would accommodate that lifestyle as well as showcase the products of their window and door manufacturing company. Located on a plateau, the slightly sloping, half-acre lot provided extensive views of the Pacific Ocean and the San Juan Islands beyond, but on a south-facing exposure that required protecting the inside living areas from direct and reflected sunlight and heat. In that sense, the porches are true transitional spaces, designed deep to control the sun exposure and other outdoor elements (mostly rain) while extending entertainment to the outside. The segmented lower porch serves the informal rooms of a walkout basement, including a game room and exercise area, while the upper porch extends from the more formal rooms of the house on that level. It's also where the family tends to spend most of its outdoor time together. We also designed the porches to compartmentalize different uses and views, primarily with the structural columns and beams, both while you're outside and when you're inside, through the windows and glass doors across the porch and out to the garden and ocean. For the home's main entry (right), we used the same materials and finishes as on the porch, creating a familiarity and a consistency in look and feel from the front to the back of the house.
—Brad Lamoureux,
MAIBC, MRAIC, principal

▲ A two-story curved-glass entry system blows through an opening in the front portico roof, delivering an element of surprise within a traditional form and creating a pavilion-like feeling. A single beam spans the opening to frame the door and bring it to a human scale.

▲ Varied ceiling treatments and heights, concrete pavers and borders, area lights, and massive columns help separate areas of the porch
without disconnecting them. The use of durable,
exterior-grade materials, finishes, and furnishings
resists occasional abuse from the elements.

Sunrise to Sunset

Porches that capture views of the sun as it breaks the horizon or as it sets behind hills, trees, or neighboring homes remind us of nature's brilliance. They showcase what can be accomplished when the gift of a sunrise, a sunset, or a view of our natural surroundings presents itself on your building site.

In contrast to the obvious goals for placement and design of porches near water, those in more general settings, from a rural forest to an urban backyard, require observation and thought, as well as inspiration. The right approach successfully connect us with nature's subtleties by framing views and connecting interior space with the outside world.

Given a choice, it's a designer's rule of thumb to try to locate a house and its porch on the spot with the best views, adding design elements to make them available for enjoyment. The implications are obvious: a porch in a forest setting, for instance, features wide openings and subtle railing treatments to put you in the trees. It aligns to track the path of the sun through the sky, and the porch faces a framed view through breaks in the tall trees of the sun setting behind the hills at the end of the day. These choices bring nature's spectacle closer, warming and brightening the porch.

A design that permits natural light and prevailing breezes to pass through the porch requires little help from artificial lighting, if any. Decide in favor of keeping the porch natural and free of unnecessary decoration. Plan and build the porch to be tolerant of a range of climate conditions. Make it deep enough to shelter the house, keep rainwater off its deck, and build it from weather-resistant materials.

When the site lacks a single dramatic view but still has ample room for a porch, turn its design inward, making the porch a more intimate, entertainment-driven space. Such porches flow out from the inside rooms, making nature a backdrop to activity instead of the center stage. Protect openings to the outside, sheltering the porch from the elements with deep overhangs and broad fascias, use solid walls and half walls instead of railings, and limit access to the porch. These details hold the eye inside the porch, a place with multiple entries to interior rooms, numerous light fixtures, and indoor-style finishes and furnishings.

The porches on the following pages show how to best take advantage of their particular settings. They offer unique solutions borne from thoughtful consideration and respect for how best to connect with nature, surroundings, and sunlight.

◄ ◄ Simple, serene, and comfortable are the cornerstone concepts for a porch or veranda designed to capture a sunrise or sunset. There's no pretense needed here, no pressure to astonish or wow; the view does that. Still, the porch reveals its own beauty, welcomes you to walk its length and find the right seat for nature's show, comforts you with basic, natural materials and finishes, evokes a true sense of security and peace of mind, and works in concert with the view.

▲ Even though the porch is nearly level with the grade, the backyard, its landscaping, and a surrounding low wall identify the porch's boundary and clearly define it as part of the home's interior space. The wall also serves double duty as a spot for casual, occasional seating.

◄◄ Using several design techniques, the architect created a fluid transition from the indoors to the porch. Each area shares the same ceiling plane and cove lighting; even the floor, while of slightly different materials and interrupted only by a door threshold, is consistent in its color hues and smooth finishes. The glass dividing wall between the porch and house features sliding doors that create a generous center opening; they further blur distinction of indoors and out.

▶ A creative lighting scheme complements the clean lines of the space. It includes contemporary-styled pendants with compelling reflections that make them appear to continue into the house, and cove lighting fixtures that actually do.

▲ Recessed light fixtures set into the solid roof eave illuminate the outdoor dining area, which links the covered and open areas of the outdoor space. The recessed light casts a diffuse glow of general illumination, which is reinforced by the double series of pendant fixtures. Note also the propane infrared space heater, used to dispel chills while dining outdoors on cool evenings.

◄ A built-in wraparound stucco counter encloses a freestanding grill, giving it the same feel as though the entire barbeque was built in. It was located at an open end of the space, where breezes flowing through the porch encourage smoke and cooking smells to be carried away from the dining area.

▶▶ A combination of stucco and concrete integrates the spaces and elements of the porch, as does a consistent use of color, which is often used instead to divide areas.

The Architect Speaks

The owners purchased this home because of its level backyard and large wooded lot, and they asked me to add a formal dining room and a guest suite off the garage wing. Plans to remodel the main house involved installing extensive exterior openings to access more light and expand its views, as well as creating a circlet of interior skylights around the raised ceilings to balance the light.

Ultimately, it was most cost effective to completely remove the main structure and rebuild it on its existing foundation with cathedral ceilings and a higher sill plate, allowing the present 8-foot-high exterior windows and doors that are keynote features of the home.

The plan resulted in raising the family room and kitchen area ceiling, which continues out onto a generous porch overlooking the backyard. These spaces, along with the open terrace along the rear of the house, work especially well together for large gatherings, accommodating guests in a variety of ways and offering them different experiences.

The porch structure uses welded steel frames called bents to keep necessary supports to a minimum, allowing the porch to remain as open as possible to the view and yard and pool beyond.

There is a serenity that comes when the materials, finishes, spaces, and furnishings are designed, coordinated, and built in a manner that is simple, clean, and straightforward.
– William Simpson,
William Simpson Architects

▲ Simple, elegant, yet comfortable furniture reinforces the porch's indoor look while complementing the clean lines of its contemporary design style. The metal-framed furnishings feature powder-coated epoxy finishes and stain-resistant fabrics to withstand the elements.

▲ Fully open, the sliding glass doors create a 6-foot-wide path to the porch. The door panels, which slide on low-profile tracks, match the fixed windows on either side, maintaining the integrity of the view and the overall effect of the design.

▶ The sliding doors are actually two independent sets, installed so the fixed panes are at opposite ends of the opening. The owners can close the doors to block weather and sound but can open them easily from either side to take full advantage of the porch. Sliders, as opposed to hinged doors, also save space.

▲ Set at one side of the home's main entrance, this arrangement around an outdoor fireplace enables family and friends to enjoy outdoor living in comfort. Wide, sturdy furniture rests easily on the porch's dry-set pavers.

▶ A see-through, wood-burning fireplace takes the chill off an evening's ocean breezes and is placed with a kitchen and outdoor dining area on the opposite side. Notice how the flagstone facing extends slightly into the firebox, giving the opening an attractively rugged and irregular appearance from the outside.

▲ Wood beams rescued from an old factory combine with stucco to create the porch's ceiling and break up the home's two-story mass (top). The covered area helps distinguish the space and draw the eye to the home's entry, while still complementing the exterior design and materials. A wide, round column with a simple capital provides a solid, classically styled anchor to the corner (bottom).

▶ Although it is set far back from the sidewalk, the home's entry is easy to find, with premade stone pavers leading the way. Folding window walls open to a second-floor terrace (above right), where 270-degree views of the ocean await.

▲ The second-story covered balcony not only frames extensive views of the ocean, but serves as a perch over the entry porch, allowing family and friends to share each other's company or see someone entering the courtyard.

▲ Lightweight elements, including a thin iron gate and fence (top) and a wood trellis for a climbing bougainvillea vine (bottom) add spots of color and contrast to the mass of the stone without competing with its influence on the home's overall design.

◄◄ Located two blocks from the ocean, the house is designed to capture coastal views and cooling breezes. The porch's design creates a breezeway across the entrance and is wide open to the front gate, inviting to both guests and gusts.

Familiar forms and finishes, from arches and barrel vaults to iron detailing, create cohesiveness, a sense of security, and soothing peace of mind. Used extensively as an outdoor retreat and gateway to the pool and olive grove, the lanai is more a covered courtyard than a conventional porch. The barrel-vaulted ceiling defines the entry and creates a sense of formality. A lack of railing makes the space appear even larger than it is, while a change in flooring pattern at the archway helps define the space and signal a step down to the pool deck and patio—an important visual cue when using similar materials. Tall sliding glass doors topped with arched transoms add to the drama and allow more light into the house.

▲ The stamped concrete floor is patterned and pigmented to appear aged, while control joints suggest stone tiles instead of a single slab. Trim around the doors matches that of the mantle and the columns, a beautiful detail that creates a sense of stability and ties the elements together.

▲ The earth tones of the lanai create a canvas that encourages stark contrasts using seasonal colors and textures.

◄◄ The fireplace is perfectly scaled for the space. It serves equally as an intimate feature or, with the furniture pulled away and its durable stainless steel frame on display, as a focal point for the entire lanai. It was a crucial feature to the lanai's design as an outdoor living area; its chair-height hearth affords extra seating, as well.

The Builder Speaks

When the acreage behind our previous home became available in subdivided lots, I jumped at the chance to build a new house that would allow our family and friends to enjoy the beauty and climate of the area.

Set in an 80-year-old olive grove, the one-acre, relatively flat site backs up to the fruit orchards and garden of my neighbor's extensive farm; closer in, we take advantage of a pool and, of course, the lanai—both of which we use at least as often as our living room.

As my architect and I considered the site and my plans for the house, we focused on the lanai to orient the house to the backyard and pool. The fireplace and dining areas create opportunities to linger there, while five sets of sliding glass doors lead to various rooms inside—including a direct line to the home's main entry. This arrangement allows parties to easily spill outdoors.

Despite its size and grandeur, the lanai is also a place to comfortably sit with a cup of coffee and the newspaper by yourself on a weekend morning, or to spend time enjoying a fire after the guests leave and the kids go to bed. It shelters us during those rare times when the weather is bad and, more commonly, provides a cool, shady spot away from the midday sun—all without forcing us indoors but rather allowing us to continue to enjoy our house and its setting.
—Steve Olsen, owner/builder

◄ Arched openings, barrel vaulted ceilings, and thick columns are common details of the Mediterranean style. The stuccoed walls and ceiling are finished in the same color, creating an effective frame that forces the eye to focus out to the view and activity instead of up at the ceiling. The design and massive materials of the lanai discourages airflow from the outside, instead creating and containing a shaded pocket of cool air for this hot, dry climate.

◄ Like the stamped concrete floor, the columns are pigmented and then stained to appear aged and weathered, as if the house had been built when the olive orchard was planted 80-some years ago. The columns not only provide structure for the deep porch, but also define openings (and barriers) to the space without requiring railings.

◄◄ With its artful arrangement of furniture, this long and deep front porch encourages conversations and community connections. Enjoyed as a true extension of the indoor living space, the porch is more a gathering area than simply a transition from the street to the house. Stone walls, thick columns, and deep eaves in the Arts & Crafts style protect the porch from sun and rain.

► The L-shaped porch wraps around one side of the home to the dining room, providing another connection to the interior and a natural place to gather after a family meal. Low-profile wicker chairs pair nicely with the stone and other porch materials, and they are fashioned with cushions designed for outdoor use.

► Original fir floors dating back to the home's construction a century ago have been refinished and sealed to retain their beauty and integrity. Area rugs serve to soften the floor and add color during summer months, while potted plants and furniture remain year-round, protected by the porch's depth from rain. The furniture and accessories, including framed art and a painted picture rail along the perimeter, combine to create the look and feel of an indoor room.

▶ The designer and homeowners updated the home's Arts & Crafts style with Asian accents and natural furniture with simple lines.

▼ In addition to ample furniture, the owner occasionally places cushions on the ledge of the stone wall for extra seating.

▶ Combining enviable summer temperatures and a wonderful outdoor shelter, the owners often host cocktail parties on their porch.

▲ This getaway, serving more as a screened house in its own right than as a room and accessed by a winding path through the woods, is set on a hilly parcel adjacent to the owner's main home in the Hill Country of Austin, Texas. Roll-up camp shades above the screened walls help control exposure to wind, sun, and rain during changes of weather, and they snap to the wood framing to simulate a vacation home's seasonal openings and closings. The main living area captures soothing views of the forest, while also revealing a dramatic peek to Austin's skyline through a fortuitous notch in the nearby hills. The floor is a composite of wood and recycled polymer, one of several low-maintenance materials used.

▲ Small sleeping quarters on either side of the fireplace designed like camp cabins with bunk beds and built-in storage, provide cozy privacy. The wood-burning fireplace delivers supplemental heat while enhancing the camp-like experience.

▶ A simple platform on concrete piers, the screened house floats on its hillside lot. An inverted roof creates a sloped gutter that captures rainwater and directs it to a cistern for irrigation. The design and orientation encourage cross breezes and natural light, but with the ability to control exposure.

▲ Wide redbrick steps and sidewalls match the foundation to stabilize the airy and ornate wrap-around porch. Equally spaced pairs of narrow columns are a much lighter touch than thick solid columns and enhance the symmetry of design elements across the front of the house.

◄ A porch of this scale requires several points of access, both from the grounds, as served by a second set of stairs to the side porch, and from the house.

▶▶ As seen here and in the photograph on this book's cover, railings, columns, and trim combine to filter light and allow summer breezes into the porch. They create a comfortable yet special place to relax and enjoy the view, whether you are standing or sitting. The matching stained wood-plank floor and ceiling, finished in a high-gloss varnish, provide an appealing contrast to the white-painted porch finishes, minimal furnishings, window frames, and clapboard siding.

▷ Details make the difference. This framed oval opening gives a glimpse of the curved rear porch while helping reduce the mass of the intricate latticework that serves as its back wall.

▷▷ A more traditional wood decking is needed to withstand the rigors of various activities on the rear porch, but its natural finish still complements the glossy plank ceiling and contrasts with the white porch details. Lattice along the back wall, mimicked in the wrought-iron furniture, creates a private enclosure from neighbors, but still allows light and refreshing breezes into and through the porch while casting interesting shadows during the day.

◁ The interior and outdoor spaces flow together almost seamlessly. Despite the prominent change in floor finishes they seem like a single living area.

▽ An extensive curved rear porch connecting two wings of the house creates a breezeway featuring interior rooms and exterior spaces along its length and multiple points of access to the pool and the house.

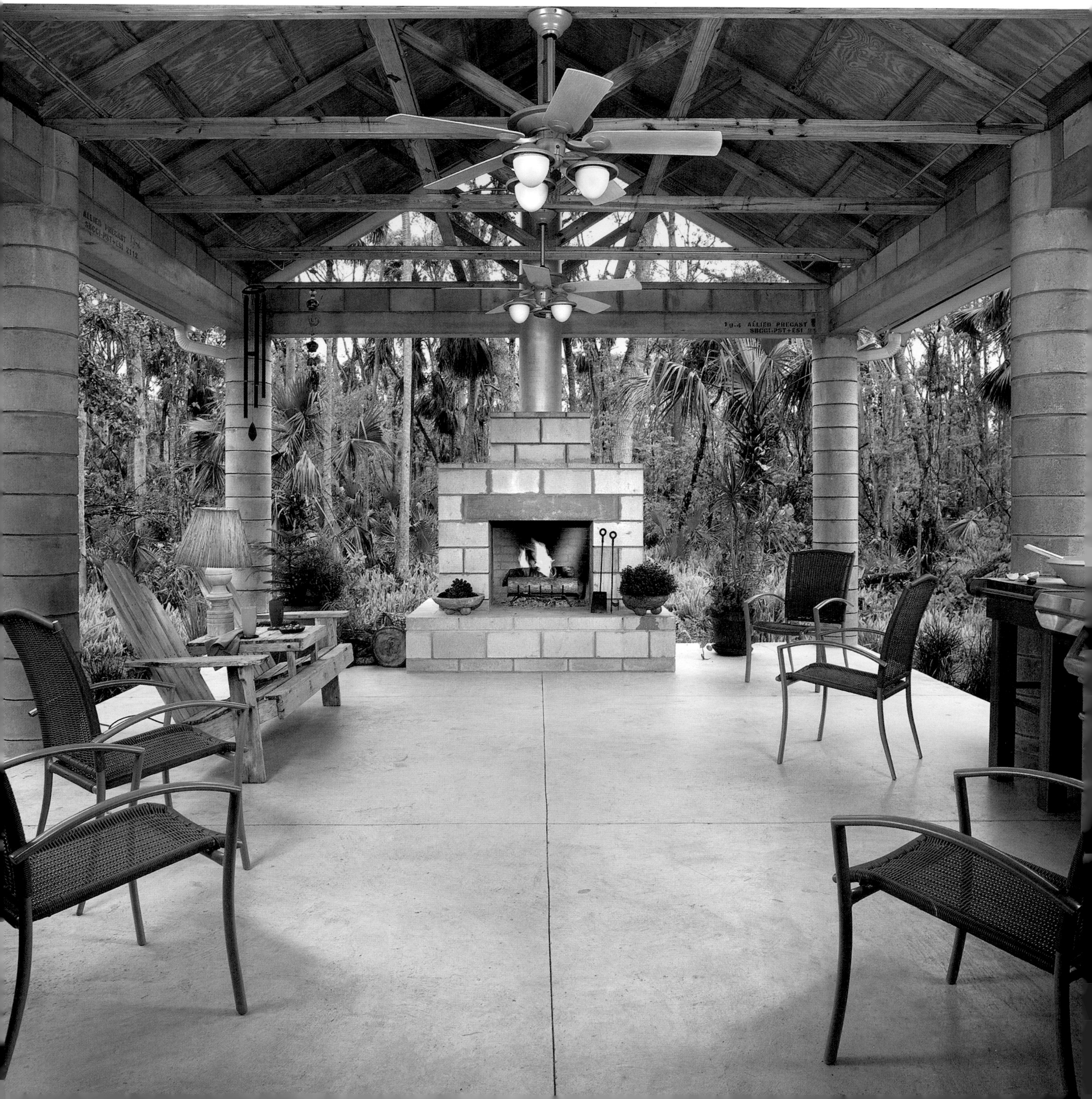
ALLIED PRECAST

▲ Instead of covering up its basic building materials such as concrete block and the roof framing, the architect-owner left them exposed to create a distinctive style—a practice that also requires more precise installation. The same materials are used inside the house, tying the indoor and outdoor rooms together. The high ceiling and open gable end reveal more of the site's natural vegetation. Ceiling fans supplement natural cross-breezes through the space.

◄◄ Akin to a picnic pavilion, the porch is open on three sides to connect it to its five-acre site and allow maximum airflow in a humid climate. The fireplace serves as a focal point, contrasting with its natural backdrop. The sealed and slip-resistant concrete slab floor features incidental impressions of leaves and ferns. The exposed roof trusses are doubled at four feet on center to create a more open frame; the roof sheathing is also doubled to 1½ inches thick so the roofing nails stay hidden on the underside.

▶ Set only one foot above grade, the porch requires no railing, which further connects it to its natural setting. A half wall toward the back conceals a gas barbecue grill and provides a bit of shelter on windy days.

▲ Designed to replicate features and details of a neighboring house built in 1911 and achieve a look that complements other dwellings located on the street, this Craftsman-style home reflects the simple lines of 1920s architecture. Notable are the subtle yet contrasting colors, a strong statement for the main entry, and a comfortable, welcoming front porch.

▲ A stone wall anchors the house to the hillside lot. It gives a sense that the house was carved out of the slope. The stone also softens and shields the sharp lines of the long, wide steps leading up to the porch. The use of white trim breaks up the gray mass, while a white beadboard ceiling reflects light into the deep porch.

◄ A sequence of landings divides the length of the front steps (far left) and makes them less daunting to climb. A rear porch and overhead deck (left) provide a perch with views and continue the front porch's look, details, and finishes.

▶ Period accessories accentuate the Craftsman style of the early 1900s.

▼ Seating areas on the second-story entry offer spectacular mountain views over the treetops.

▶▶ Walking by the porch's informal gathering area on your way to the front door makes a comfortable transition from the street into the house. The porch is deep enough to allow a generous amount of furniture, encouraging conversation while retaining a free passageway. A single pendant light signals your arrival at the home's front entry.

▼ The indirect staircase up to the front door meant choosing a distinctive and contrasting finish and style to clearly identify the door from the street. Within the Craftsman-style of the house, the use of a darker, heavier wood and flanking sidelites makes the main entry obvious.

◄◄ A quintessential example of blended indoor and outdoor space, this dining porch features arched-stone openings that frame views like pieces of art. Sandstone walls, a cypress-paneled ceiling, and a limestone floor strongly identify this porch as an outdoor space, as does its exterior-grade wall sconces, with a dedicated use more akin to an interior dining room. Its stone walls are slow to warm or lose Texas' heat, moderating the temperatures inside the room.

▶ One of several covered porches and outdoor areas along the home's sprawling rear elevation (below right), the space provides access to the kitchen through a simple pair of wood-framed glass doors centered on the wide archway and has steps that lead to the back lawn and meadow garden. The steps, arch, doors, and windows on the second floor reduce the mass of the stone structure to an intimate human scale, making the porch both inviting and comfortable.

◄ Door and window cutouts provide function and form, promoting cross breezes on hot summer nights and framing glimpses of surrounding nature. A nod to interior design features, the fireplace within the room employs similar materials to those used for the porch, blending them in to avoid dominating the space.

▲ Keeping to classic Victorian styling, the deep wraparound porch of this mountain retreat is adorned with appropriate ornamentation. Though extensive, the slender elements keep the effect light and airy, adding an attractive fringe to the porch and contrast with the blue clapboard siding. Notice how the dark handrail nicely ties the balustrade with the steps, lattice, and decking.

◀◀ The thin-column theme is repeated in the porch rail the top spindles, framing extensive views of the farm and mountains beyond. The rural location has great privacy despite two nearby roads, and the porch was designed to be hidden from view on two sides.

▶ The porch affords several areas for different functions as its wraps around the house, including a generous outdoor dining spot, space for comfortable contemplation, and ample room for whimsical accessories that enhance the overall style of the porch and home.

Linger Here

The urban front porch's more active setting, often with its close proximity to sidewalks and street traffic, requires a design to deliver that city-neighborhood connection with the same sure certainty that would be found in a natural setting's thick forest or lake. In typically urban or suburban settings, porches connect you to your neighbors and the neighborhood, forging a conduit from the private life inside your house to the public concourse of the sidewalk and street. It's a place to meet, greet, and engage with passersby, and it becomes a vital player in the rediscovery of what fosters community.

The design objective is a dedicated effort to invite and welcome people onto the porch, which becomes a transitional space between the neighborhood and your house. It may have a pair of chairs, a bench swing, or a glider, usually reserved for your personal use, or it may be more elaborately appointed, encouraging lengthy conversations.

To accomplish the task, push the porch out as far as possible toward the street, reducing to more human scale the otherwise undifferentiated face and mass of a multistory building. Center the approach on the front door—usually with steps or stairs, but sometimes with porch-wide tiers—or clearly direct visitors to other points of access.

Such porches welcome neighborly relationships but maintain a semblance of privacy. Often they face the street and must be open and inviting to visitors, but they must also provide security; an ideal porch offers a place to sit and people-watch, greet your neighbors, and witness their activity while protecting you and your home's interior.

Options allow you to enjoy the positives yet mitigate the negatives. Screens on a porch give you the enjoyment of the sights and sounds of nature but keep out pests and debris; skylights capture natural light and provide unobstructed overhead views while protecting from rain or snow; modern synthetics make porches easy to maintain, yet appear as authentic as their natural counterparts, maintaining a sense of tradition.

As alternatives to front porches, sunrooms provide still another option for urban or suburban locales. Completely enclosed, yet encompassing an outdoor setting, they are the right choice for homes with limited street setbacks but generous side- or backyards.

The porches and sunrooms featured here showcase what can be done to nurture community connections, provide places for contemplation, and offer safe havens where you can come to know your neighbors as friends.

◄◄ With its classic forms and features, patterned brick deck, and comfortable depth, this front porch in Orlando recalls early American architecture. Set among a row of like-sized homes, the house overlooks a mews—a common-space park—shared by its neighbors. It encourages connections and provides security. With its span across the entire front of the house and door mid-porch, it has room for multiple furnishings and two conversation areas; its ample depth protects cushions, linens, and accessories from afternoon thunderstorms. Additional photographs of this project continue on the overleaf, pages 110–111.

◀ Inviting front porches encourage neighborhood connections and enable interaction with folks enjoying the mews that fronts by this and another row of houses across the way—a revival of the densely sited homes and diverse styling that cropped up near urban areas in the first half of the 20th century.

▶ With elements consistent with its classic Spanish roots, most notably a trio of arched openings, this house and porch are a stark departure from the traditional American porch next door. A bit more formal in its feel and decor, the porch also acts as an entry colonnade. Though wraparound stone stairs allow entrance at any opening, the porch does not feel exposed or unprotected, thanks to its depth and bulk.

◀◀ The choice of materials, finishes, lighting, and other details create a sense of formality on this porch without sacrificing comfort. Although open and inviting to the common park, the porch's integral design with the rest of the house offers a more private and intimate space. Each of the three archways leading out of the porch is replicated with a subtle detail over the arched doors into the house; notice how the color and texture of the solid-wood front door contrasts with the window-like treatment of the patio door framed in the next arch, clearly identifying the home's entry while allowing ample access, light, and views into and from the interior rooms along the front of the house.

▶ True to its architectural heritage, this porch (also seen on page 108) centers on the home's front entry with generous areas on either side for conversation, relaxation, and even casual meals. A brick porch deck spills out on the steps and walk to anchor the home, adds color and dimension, and clearly indicates the path to the front door. The railings and shrubs, especially on either end of the porch, provide subtle screens to the close-knit neighborhood.

Despite its generous depth and length, this huge wraparound porch maintains a casual, welcoming feel with a low ceiling and an open railing. Wide staircases on the ends lead to the two street frontages of the home's corner lot.

▶▶ Naturally stained shingle siding balances the austerity of the floor and white beadboard ceiling, which might appear uninviting otherwise. The full-width stairs prepare you for the breadth of the porch.

▼ Turned from the street, the main entry is easily reached by two sets of stairs. Potted plants and furniture help soften the sharp lines and hard surfaces of the porch's floor and ceiling.

▲ A rust-colored planter with a dwarf red-leaved Japanese maple is complementary to the home's natural shingle exterior. It dresses the porch's corner as it transitions to the steps.

▲ The deep overhang, extended even beyond the thick, rounded columns, shelters the main entry and the side entry around the corner, as well as the windows and furnishings along its length. The various textures, colors, and detailing on this porch combine for a beautiful composition that commands attention from the street but also welcomes—and protects—you when you venture onto it or simply imagine yourself enjoying its comforting embrace.

As twilight begins its fade into dusk, three symmetrical overhead lamps cast a warm glow on the porch's ceiling, walls, columns, and railing.

▲ Massive columns spaced evenly along the length of the main porch deliver a proportion and rhythm that perfectly suit the porch, while cascading side stairs anchor the porch to the lot.

▶ Railings enclose the space to maintain scale. Simple stiles, spaced widely apart and bounded by a gracefully molded handrail, tease the eye with glimpses of the landscape and yard.

◄ Returned to its original and historically accurate design, this porch received an award from a local historical society. A previous owner had enclosed the porch, making it into a room within the house. After restoration, it again functions as it was first designed. The grandson of the woodcrafter who made the original columns milled several new pillars to match those that survived. The porch sets right up to the sidewalk, conjuring images in the mind of tightly woven European neighborhoods.

◄ The solid wall creates a barrier to the street, blocking views into the house, while the combination of colors, casual furnishings, hanging and potted plants, and charming details welcome interaction. The design employs a gated side entry and inset steps, reserving the center of the porch for a seating area rather than functioning as a passageway to the front entry.

▲ True to its roots, the porch features Craftsman details such as exposed eaves, austere columns, and a paneled ceiling. The Mediterranean climate of long and dry but foggy summers and rainy winters found in Pacific Grove, California, make the roof's wide overhang a practical feature for the porch. It shelters the porch's deck from wind-blown mists and rains during storms.

▶ Entering from the side instead of directly from the street, visitors enjoy the full extent of the porch and its neighborhood views before making their way inside.

◄ Subtle details, from the exposed rafter tails of the roof to the continuation of the columns and cutouts on the wall reduce, the mass of the solid porch wall. A narrow gap in the wall features a slight drip edge and allows the owner to sweep water and debris off the porch.

▲ The owner's pair of friendly Airedales find the porch's half-wall height ideal for perching at the sidewalk's edge, as they wait for a kind word and a pat as neighbors pass by.

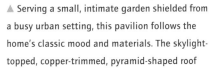 Serving a small, intimate garden shielded from a busy urban setting, this pavilion follows the home's classic mood and materials. The skylight-topped, copper-trimmed, pyramid-shaped roof shelters a portico that gives dual access from the interior of the home to the outdoors.

◄◄ Columns set into the brickwork convey strength at the corners to balance the room's openness while also conserving valuable space. Granite-topped stucco steps lead to the garden.

▶ An oasis for the owners, the garden room receives light filtered from the trees as well as from the skylight above, which was designed to capture unobstructed views of the sky.

While distinctive in its design, the screened porch maintains the basic lines and forms of the main structure. Set at midlevel on the corner of a 1970s split-level house, the porch's skirt of a deck and stairs shields its foundation. The architects added a bump-out window and French doors to the home's existing gable end to reduce the mass of the clapboard siding and better complement the porch's more open design.

A narrowing of the steps that lead to the setback doors focuses the eye on their location. Modest materials and details, including boxed columns, newel posts, and a consistent railing height, create crisp lines that are in character with the rest of the house.

Designed to allow the owners to enjoy the outdoors on late afternoons and evenings protected from pests, this screened porch uses board-and-batten walls, a painted beadboard ceiling, exposed beams, and mahogany decking to create an outdoor feel. The white walls and ceiling serve to reflect both natural and artificial light, making the porch feel light and airy inside.

A mahogany deck and steps, stretched across the width of the screened porch and its entry landing, spill gracefully to a brick terrace and the backyard beyond. The broad steps provide enough space for outdoor seating and give a gentle approach to the house suited to its slightly sloping lot.

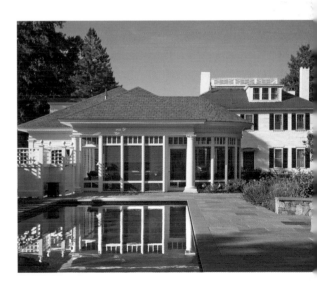

▲ Having added a carriage-style garage that suited the home's historic Federal style, the owners also wanted a seasonal space that would orient them to the backyard pool.

◄ Cove lighting recessed into the thick crown moulding of the screened porch's interior creates a soothing ambient light that extends out to the pool deck. Square-set slate tiles are another shared feature, further connecting the pool to its seasonal partner.

▲ Designed solely for summer use, the screened porch puts a respectful—if less formal—spin on the home's Federal-style details and forms.

▲ Mullions add detail to the top of the screened openings; the lower rail offers structural support, balance, and a visual cue. The openings frame the landscaped yard beyond the pool.

▲ A curved bump-out captures a greater view of the long, narrow lot while also helping define the dining area inside. The placement of the door is critical to efficient traffic flow indoors.

► Dense mahogany enabled the use of narrow framing members for the screened openings.

The Architect Speaks

When the owners decided to build a carriage-style garage to serve this historic home, the plan also included construction of a screened-porch addition that would serve as a summer living area when the pool was in use—an alternative to a seasonal second home somewhere else and a magnet for family and friends to gather. Instead of starting with a blank slate and unlimited options, we enjoy drawing upon what's unique about an historic house. The design evolves naturally from what's already there, yet is still harmonious. Because the porch was shielded from view, we had a little more latitude in its design (the curved section is especially playful), as opposed to the rigid standards of the garage. We were also mindful of its connection to the house. We made sure to include elements like deep-profile mountings inside and out, to replicate the slope of the home's hipped roof, and to borrow subtle references to the mullioned windows on the porch's screened openings. To maximize the amount of screened area, we chose mahogany as our framing material. Resistant to the weather, this dense hardwood allowed us to use smaller-dimension members to frame the openings without sacrificing structural integrity. The effect is a porch that truly gives you the feeling of being outdoors, but in the comfort of a protected indoor space.

—William Soupcoff, AIA, principal

▲ Taking advantage of a long, narrow lot, the screened porch dedicates a full kitchen, living area, and dining room to the family's seasonal enjoyment of its pool and garden. Like the pool, the porch is shut down for the winter, closed off from the rest of the house until pleasant weather returns.

Twin columns, in homage to the main home's historic style, support a protective overhang in front of the doors nested to each side of the central screened wall. Lines and proportions are consistent across the entire rear elevation and between the screened openings and doors, tying the elements together.

Designed and Refined

Furnishing your porch or sunroom brings your interior design skills and material choices to an under-roof space that is essentially part of an outdoor setting. Dividing up the porch's space, selecting flooring and window covering materials, furnishing each area, adding artificial lighting, and decorative accents—the customary issues of interior decoration—move to the forefront as dealing with architectural plans and construction phases begin to wind down.

Use your design professional as a resource as you begin the process of outfitting your porch. During planning, the designer considered how sunlight and other natural illumination would fall on the porch, established sheltered areas free of wind and rain, and oriented the porch to capture a view or permit close involvement with your neighbors. Sketches and drawings may suggest placements of furniture, detail fixtures, and offer color themes. Add your own ideas to these now that you can walk on your porch and understand its scale.

Start by planning how you will utilize the porch and who will use it. Do you plan to relax on it, dine or converse with friends, or will it be a recreation area for children? Will it be a space for adults, family, or elders? Each use you intend and each type of user has an impact the details of its furnishings.

The goal is to visualize how the porch will be used in a variety of situations, and where each of those uses will take place. Flesh out your thinking by considering the major furniture and fixtures the porch will require to achieve each purpose. For a diminutive porch, think of small-space solutions: moveable storage cabinets and trunks, folding tables and chairs, portable lamps; multiple functions are important in such cases. For larger areas, divide the space into rooms, each with its own, sometimes overlapping, uses.

Next, look at the built-in amenities. If the porch has a cooking area with a barbecue, set aside an area for food preparation and serving and choose a nearby eating area. If your porch has a fireplace, maximize your enjoyment of it with seating options, and set aside space for them. If the porch is located near a swimming pool, deck, or patio, their use may affect the functions of the porch. Spend time on your porch and note how the sunlight falls on it, where breezes flow through its openings, and decide where artificial lighting or additional wind protection will be needed.

◄◄ Outdoor sitting rooms are protected under the overhang of a porch and extend the living area of a house beyond its walls to include the outdoors. Furnishings, fabrics, and colors help integrate each outdoor room with its surroundings, while defining areas for various activities, whether it be sharing an intimate conversation, relaxing before a fireplace, or eating a meal.

▶ Outfitting the porch as a seating area with comfortable, weather-tolerant furnishings and decorative plants accentuates the dramatic visual planes of the open ceiling and massive frame and trusses, uniting the indoor and outdoor rooms into a cohesive and inviting space.

▲ Draw interest to a casual seating area with a dramatic half-circle window, barrel-vaulted ceilings, and angular planes for the screen frames.

Having settled on a purpose, who will use your porch, and its overall space plan, take a look at how it makes the transition into your home. Very likely, the design and construction team's effort included details and elements—arches, windows, doorways, and trimwork—that integrate the porch or sunroom with the adjacent rooms of the house. Areas of a porch off of an entry foyer will function differently from those found next to a kitchen, family room, or dining room. Emphasize the relationship by choosing furnishings that complement or stand apart from those of the home's interior. If you plan to extend the use of the interior room onto the porch, the transitional elements and furnishings are essential to achieving a quality result.

While decor in an outdoor porch or sunroom might be a subject worthy of its own book, distinctive treatments and decorative concepts illustrate the principles of porch furnishing. In the following pages, you will find examples of the major furnishing components: walls and window coverings, flooring and floor coverings, porch furniture, lighting fixtures and occasional lamps, and potted plants.

▲ From its deck-like floor and rustic furnishing to its massive stone fireplace and floor-to-ceiling screened window openings, this spacious porch retains nearly all of its outdoor-space character, yet it provides shelter from the elements for year-round enjoyment.

▶ Even with a deep overhang to protect against direct sunlight, open porches facing the sun may require window coverings to block glare and heat gain. A simple solution is roll-up, exterior-grade split bamboo or fabric shades. Another option is wood or synthetic shutters. Either provides a tough, weather-resistant shield to block heat and direct sunlight from entering the home's interior.

WALLS AND WINDOW COVERINGS

The first order of business is color: choose a paint, stain, or wash for the walls, or apply facing brick or stone to match similar elements on the house. Ceilings, whether open-beam or finished, are best treated with light colors that will gather every bit of the light they receive, diffuse it, and reflect it downward as glowing soft light. Warm tones amplify the effect, while cool hues make the porch more inviting at midday in hot climates.

It is traditional for back walls to match the house's existing paint or siding, but use light-colored complementary finishes for the side walls and the insides of half walls—they'll appear more like interior walls—and vary the trimwork finishes on the inside of the porch from the main structure. For masonry and shingle facings, choose the lightest finish compatible with the house. On walls, avoid dark wood treatments except for Arts and Crafts– or Tudor-style homes, where they should match the original detailing choices; in such cases, apply light trim colors to moderate the facing's impact and add visual interest; make the mouldings and fascias wider than is typical in other styling situations.

If the wall between the house and porch includes windows, choose similar sill and trim treatments for both the interior and exterior faces. Control light to south-facing interiors with exterior shutters, blinds, or drapery walls made of weatherproof fabric, hung either at the windows or in the porch openings. Natural wood is a good option, as are neutral colors, or select a window treatment with light and dark tones on its alternate faces so it will reflect light away or hold and absorb warmth as the situation demands.

Retractable shades and awnings are practical additions to sunrooms and sun porches enclosed with glass. While these spaces are inviting in the morning, they tend to bake in the noonday sun. Reflective films applied to their glass surfaces and barriers made of shade fabric help moderate a sunroom's greenhouse-like tendencies, and the shade-cloth panels add dramatic color to contrast with the sky or scenes viewed behind the windows.

▶▶ Sunrooms offer full views of the sky and yard, but they sometimes overheat because they trap infrared radiation within their glass walls. Shield the room from the sun's midday heat with motorized, exterior-rated fabric shades on tracks mounted to the metal framing, and control them with temperature-sensing systems.

▲ Traditional masonry finishes such as brick, stone, or ceramic tiles anchor a porch to its surroundings. Masonry is a durable and stable floor that tolerates exposure to the elements and acts as a heat sink to slowly warm or cool the porch, moderating its temperature.

FLOORING AND FLOOR COVERINGS

A wide selection of flooring options exists for both remodeled and newly built porches. Masonry floors include simple unfinished, stamped or skim-coated concrete, or natural stone, brick, ceramic tile, and mosaic, among other options. Wood floors may be made of simple deck-like lumber, finished tongue-and-groove wood-strip hardwood, plank, or parquet. Sheet linoleum or linoleum tiles—suited to some weather-exposed conditions—or exterior carpet are other options for porches.

Safety, practicality, climate and livability should all be considered when choosing a floor material. Dew or rain exposure is a fact of life for porches, and the best surface choices are skid resistant when wet, avoid staining, and are easily cleaned. On painted wood floors, choose durable epoxy finishes, and add skid-resistant grit for greater safety. Grouted joints require sealing and regular renewal to prevent moisture from penetrating to the subfloor and supporting frame, causing decay. Because sunlight will hit the floor and

◀ Wood strips or planks are other options for finishing a porch floor. To maintain their good looks and structural integrity, protect the wood from the elements by designing the porch with a broad overhang to block rain, and finish the floor with several coats of protective urethane epoxy or marine-rated varnish.

▼ A concrete slab, typically seen in at- or near-grade porches, provides an economical and low-maintenance flooring solution. Dress up the slab with stamped patterns or use it as a neutral canvas for colorful throw rugs and typical outdoor furniture.

reflect up, avoid glare by using darker colors and warmer hues. Outdoor furniture, popular for most porches, is constantly rearranged for cleaning and entertaining; a porch floor should be level and made from hard, and scratch-free materials. Screened porches and sunrooms with minimal exposure to rain are the best candidates for indoor-outdoor carpet.

Consider dressing up a plain slab-masonry floor from its plain-Jane, gray state with a carefully applied concrete stain. Unique, attractive, and artful effects are possible with borders stained in patterns that contrast with the field areas of the flooring. When used in combination with skim-coat stamping, the effect can mimic laid stone, parquet, mosaic, and other complex finishes at a fraction of their budget.

Also add color and define sections of the porch's floor with area rugs made of easy-to-clean natural fibers such as cotton, jute, sisal, or wool. Rugs stand out from the neutral fields of a hardwood or concrete floor. Place them where they are compatible with the porch's intended use, such as under a bistro table in a pool of warm morning sunlight. Mount rugs on slip-proof backings on smooth surfaces, or use them to level uneven masonry floor.

PORCH FURNITURE

The layout and structure of a porch dictate in great part how its furnishings will be arranged. It is doubly important, therefore, that you and your design team agree from the beginning on how you plan to use each area of the porch. Ask your design professional to suggest furniture options based on the area's function, from lounging and reading to socializing and dining, and solicit comments about the suitability of furniture that appeals to you.

Use furnishings—tables, chairs, chaise lounges, gliders, hammocks, hassocks, and the like—as flexible additions to a porch's or sunroom's amenities, knowing that they may serve for a time and then be replaced. Permanent fixtures, by contrast, should be placed first, during the construction phase, where they will achieve the effect required; these include suspended porch swings, overhead fans, fireplaces, grills, sinks, and other built-in appliances. (Lighting fixtures, outlets, and switches have similar characteristics, and will be dealt with in the following section).

Assemble furniture and fixture groupings to define and divide the space on your porch. Evaluate traffic flow through the porch, making passage easy and direct to entry points leading to the yard or to the interior of the house. Keep activity areas out of the traffic patterns, or direct the traffic by how you place the furniture and use each area. Emphasize views through furniture placement, and dress low-use areas and corners with appealing decorative items or use them to park moveable serving carts and other items.

Decide whether an eating area will be used for a casual snack and drink, an intimate dinner for two, a gathering of family and friends, or shared food preparation as well as serving. Choose and arrange furniture for seating areas by making it suitable for either relaxed lounging, group conversations, or active participation and games. Select tables in scale to the porch's dimensions, and experiment with their placement.

Use your knowledge of the porch's lighting, airflow, and sheltered spots to plan how each area will be used. The porch's best views may well be from spots that would receive blowing rain during a storm, so keep them open and use them as traffic corridors. Set tables and seating areas back from the front edge, increasing their protection from the elements, while making them inviting and practical.

▶▶ A generous veranda offers ample space for multiple furniture sets. Furnishings divide the covered space into individual rooms, from groups around the dual hearth of the fireplace and television to intimate lounges and places to eat. All are arranged to allow an easy traffic flow in, around, and through the veranda.

▲ Outdoor furniture placed on a covered porch or within a sunroom breaks up dominant colors or surfaces. Synthetic wicker, besides being resistant to mold and weathering, is usually light enough to easily rearrange into new positions for flexibility in entertaining.

Most furniture made for outdoor use—lawns, patios, and decks—is also well suited for a porch or sunroom. Such pieces are weather resistant, lightweight and easily moved, long-lasting, and attractive. Synthetic materials and epoxy finishes don't have most of the problem-causing features found in wood, wicker, rattan, and fabric, such as mold, checking, discoloration, and fading. These natural materials retain their charm if you are willing to maintain them. Furniture of a tropical wood such as teak, for instance, will retain its show-room appearance if it's regularly oiled and stored indoors during the winter. For a more natural look in a beachside setting, allow it to weather to silver gray.

For high-exposure locations, choose pieces made of anodized aluminum or powder-coated metal; they shed rain and wipe clean with soapy water. Place a few ventilated teak boxes or trunks on the porch for storing upholstered cushions for sofas and lounge or occasional chairs. The appearance of such furniture changes dramatically through use of

▶ Two revitalized versions of a classic theme: use porch swings to close off the area's end and mark an edge, supplementing a railing or replacing it for an on-grade porch (top). A deep, wide bench is essential (bottom); set the height of the swing to make it easily accessible and comfortable to users of every age.

colorful patterned fabrics and throw pillows, and these accessories are economical choices for quickly and inexpensively changing your porch furniture's appearance. Fabric throws serve the same purpose, and they have the added benefit of warding off the chilly night air when guests linger in the evening.

Unless the porch is expansive, choose loveseats instead of sofas and pick similarly compact upholstered chairs rather than their full-sized cousins. The same considerations apply to gliders and bench swings: it's better for them to fit two persons comfortably than to offer more seating but use up valuable porch space. Will a round table for four be a better choice than a rectangular piece that sits six or eight? Perhaps, but if your goal is to entertain larger groups with outdoor meals, the larger piece might be necessary (better yet, choose one that is expandable). Remember occasional tables and hassocks. They're useful places to set a glass and plate when dining from a buffet or barbecue, and they'll hold a book or give you a place to rest your feet while taking up little space.

Choose multifunctional furniture, including hammocks, rockers, gliders, and drop-leaf tables or serving carts on casters. These pieces are welcome additions to most porches. They replace larger lounges, dining chairs, and tables, take up a fraction of their space, and can be stored in out-of-the way corners or off the porch between uses. Unless you plan to cook regularly on your porch, a portable propane grill is a smarter, space-efficient choice.

For a protected and private porch on a second level, or for a porch or veranda intended to serve a bedroom, dining room, or kitchen, join the porch and its companion interior room with coordinated furnishings and encourage indoor-outdoor seasonal living. For such use, the indoor room's furniture should tend to a more casual, comfortable, and relaxed treatment instead of a traditional look, helping it to reflect and function in tandem with its porch counterpart: choose wicker and rattan island-style furniture and natural jute or sisal area rugs, for instance. Continue these themes on the porch with a wicker daybed instead of a sofa, offering the suggestion of the porch as a cool sleeping place for warm, humid nights. Hang drapes of cotton gauze as window or patio-door treatments to rustle in the breeze, flowing between and visually joining the two rooms.

Furnishing is a balancing act between planning and satisfying your down-to-earth intent and romantic yearnings. These choices will personalize your space and make it your own.

▲ Choose porch furniture with a style, materials, and finish to blend with and complement the porch's design and that of your house. Protect the furniture from weather by storing it indoors during the winter, or allow it to age gracefully.

Another common porch situation is placement of a seating area just off a front entry door. Many porches are extensions of the home's front elevation, with a seating area to one or both sides of the front door. This naturally divides the porch into one or more casual sitting areas, and invites the use of a suitably scaled loveseat or a pair of armchairs and a coffee table. In larger-scale porches, there may be room for both chairs and a sofa, but the character of the space lends itself to enjoyment by a small number of people engaged in casual conversation, rather than as an activity area for dining or playing games, or a place to entertain larger groups.

Make such locations functional by choosing comfortable seating as well as focusing on the style of the ensemble. Comfort depends on three considerations: height of seat, depth of cushion, and back support. Each individual is unique, so avoid one-size-fits-all solutions. The height of the seat is adjustable by providing different cushion thicknesses, but the space from the front to the back of the cushion is determined by the piece's back construction;. an overly deep seat means that guests must perch forward from the backrest. Backrests with curved lumbar support are more comfortable than straight-backed chairs and sofas.

When you find seating that fits your body, style, and objectives, match the coffee and end tables to it, noting how the pieces fit your space and work together. The result will be a comfortable place to meet and greet friends. To accommodate occasional larger groups, keep a reserve of folding chairs in an indoor closet or a storage area under the porch.

As you can see from the examples of a few special situations, giving thoughtful consideration to your needs—and those of your guests and family—means that you'll still have many furnishing options from which to choose. You'll customize your porch and express your creativity by treating each element of its furnishings with the attention that it deserves.

For those with toddlers or young children, a protected porch is an inviting place to play. Precaution dictates that you provide added security for them by planning ahead for their safety and appropriately furnishing and equipping the porch with added features. Consider large area rugs to soften falls on hard, rough masonry or unyielding wood floors. Choose tables, chairs, and other pieces of furniture that are low, wide, and stable, and pick designs with rounded rather than sharp corners. Set tables or carts in front of pane-glass windows or replace them with tempered glass. And, for the very young, use pressure-locked guard gates at each entry point, especially on porches above grade.

▲ If you have the space, mix different styles of furniture for different uses, such as socializing, lounging, napping, reading, and dining. Deep, cushioned teak chairs (above left) are suited to short periods on the porch. An upholstered armchair and hassock (above), by comparison, are the right choices for hours of pleasurable reading interrupted only by a quick casual meal served to family at the dining table behind it.

▶ Pendant and hanging light fixtures require high ceilings with plenty of headroom. Unusual overhead fixtures accent the character of a porch at night, making it more akin to an interior space.

▼ Choose table lamps for supplemental lighting. They are easily relocated, illuminate details, provide direct light for tasks, and spill indirect light on walls, ceilings, and floors.

PORCH-LIGHTING FIXTURES AND LAMPS

Proper lighting is important for any porch, allowing you to extend a porch's use into the evening hours. Well-planned lighting transforms a porch, giving it an entirely different appearance at dusk and into the night than it has during the daytime. Like the interior of your home, provide for a variety of lighting. Include permanent light fixtures in your design plans, and allow for occasional lamps.

Have your design professional specify both permanent overhead and wall-mounted light fixtures and include provision for ample shock-protected ground-fault-circuit interrupter outlets around the porch's perimeter; they're a necessity for exposed locations. Plan for chandeliers and pendant lamps with ceiling heights that lift the installed fixture at least six feet eight inches above the floor or, in low-ceiling areas, use overhead track, can, recessed, or indirect lighting fixtures.

The photographs in this book show many porches with well-planned lighting systems, but some vintage porches lack adequate lighting—like a 1950s kitchen with only a central overhead light—and need to be modernized with adequate overall and task lighting fixtures. The right combination of fixtures, bulbs, controlling switches, and placement means every part and function of the porch will be illuminated properly.

As you plan, choose lighting fixtures that fit the period and style of your home; they're just one of the many details that will tie together into your porch's entire design palette. Use dimmer switches to control the amount of light that each fixture emits, and choose energy-saving, long-lasting bulbs. These options are especially important for fixtures with multiple bulbs.

Depending on how it is cast and with what intensity, light can illuminate, mottle, or emphasize the texture of the surface on which it shines. Pick the right fixtures for the right situation. Some lights feature groups or series of several small bulbs rather than a central fixture; they cast multiple, overlapping points of brightness and textured shadows that are pleasing to the eye. Mount downlights in the overheads above work surfaces, such as a cooktop or grill, but avoid their use in sitting areas; individuals caught in their spotlight will find the emphasis uncomfortable. Instead—especially on porches that have open-beam ceilings—use indirect lighting cast upward and reflected down onto the seating area. The same effect can be achieved with wall sconces, which suffuse light up the wall on which they are mounted. Remember to specify step lighting for your stairs to increase their visibility at night and enhance safety.

Once your permanent fixtures and furnishings are in place, you'll note some spots that need supplemental lighting. Use occasional floor and table lamps to add illumination to these locations. Choose translucent shades that block glare from people seated at eye level, but cast light downward and up to bounce it off the ceiling. The result will be pockets and pools of brightness amid areas of lower, yet adequate illumination.

Match lamps to your other furnishings. Lamp bases come in a wide range of materials, from basketry and pottery to wrought iron, chrome, and brass. Choose shades to match nearby furniture made from the same or complementary materials. Compose groups of lamps around a unifying theme such as vining plants or nautical elements.

All of the fixtures and lamps used on a weather-exposed porch must be safety-rated for outdoor use and must include sealed switches. Because adding lighting to decks and patios is popular, there are many outdoor options from which to choose; if in doubt, consult with your design team or an outdoor lighting specialist.

▲ For eye-level and overhead lighting, chandeliers (left), sconces (center), and pendant fixtures (right) are to be found in many styles, finishes, and materials. Each has its place on the right porch, veranda, or sunroom. Coordinate the styles and materials of permanent lighting fixtures and occasional lamps to achieve the best look for your outdoor room.

Wreaths and pots or baskets, either in groups (below), or alone and filled with flowering plants (right), provide a finishing touch to porch decor. Make them a centerpiece, or fill inside and outside corners of the porch with plants and sculptural groupings.

FOLIAGE AND FLOWERING PLANTS

Living plants and flowers—or their dried or artificial counterparts—along with many other decorator items, are the finishing touches to your well-appointed porch or sunroom. They bring grace notes to enjoying it as an outdoor room. Because a porch is subject to the same weather conditions as your surrounding yard, cut flowers from your garden are an obvious first choice for adding color. If the space receives strong winds, arrange them in bottom-heavy vases or place them in a stable and tightly fitting plant stand to prevent them from tipping. You'll likely find that they last a bit longer than their indoor counterparts owing to the better light and natural temperatures they experience on your porch.

Potted plants are the interior designer's choice for adding enduring texture, color, and patterns to any space. Choose from either flowering plants—knowing you'll have to swap them out when their blooms fade—or the many foliage plants, from palms to evergreens and topiaries. With all living plants, watering is necessary, so plant them in well-drained containers placed in waterproof cache pots. The cache pot can be hidden within an outer pot, container, or basket, and it will collect water drained from the plant during watering and protect your porch floor from flooding and staining.

Any plant becomes a sculptural presence on the porch. Choose from tall, wide, or bushy species, depending on your needs. Allow foliage to drape over the porch railing or wall, or fill an opening with a tall plant. Make groups of planted and empty containers—

Use a tall, leafy plant as a divider to shield nearby houses from view, adding privacy to the porch. Consider how greenery, topiaries, and other potted plants will affect the views of the porch from the curb, from on the porch itself, even from within the house through a window. Select porch furnishings made of natural materials such as wicker, cane, or wood, or pick those upholstered with light, waterproof cotton cloth.

For seasonal color, plantings of annual flowers, grasses, even decorative kale, fill a pot or planter box and make it a foundation for color and texture on the porch.

odd numbered sets of threes or fives are visually pleasing—and fill an unused inside corner of the porch with them. The combination of pot and flower colors, foliage patterns, and textures gives many options for adding color, texture, or warmth to your space.

Choose locations for your porch's plants and furniture that can be seen from inside your home, or ones that frame a view through its windows. Coordinate your porch with your home's overall appearance by choosing a decor and furnishings that invite you and your family and friends to visit and linger there each time you or they pass by.

Detail by Detail

One of the great mysteries of modern construction is how a design on paper is transformed into reality. Despite being on public display at every work site, the building process is usually confusing and cryptic, complete with a language all its own. As the owner, it's your responsibility to gain a basic understanding of the process as it specifically relates to your porch project, from the type of foundation and framing system to the windows and trimwork; you'll be involved right down to the last detail.

While the job may seem daunting at first, the results of your efforts will be a more intimate knowledge of your house and porch, a greater respect for proper maintenance, and a deeper appreciation for the work and decisions required to build it. You'll develop a better relationship with your design professional and contractor, becoming a true member of the team instead of simply the client, relied upon and trusted for your input and insight toward creating a space that enhances your quality of life and the value of your property.

This chapter is designed to take you step-by-step through a short course on the basics of porch construction. You'll gain insight into the sometimes subtle but no less critical differences between new construction and a remodeling project, as well as converting or adapting a porch space for different seasons and uses. You'll also learn the variety of structural systems available for your porch project and why certain systems and materials are chosen, all depending on the porch's location, the site and soil conditions, your budget, and design considerations.

Once the structural work is finished, it's time to complete the porch. In addition to choosing basic materials for finishing its floor, ceiling, and walls, you must make a number of important decisions regarding the lighting plan, windows, and decorative trimwork, and you'll decide how all of those elements will be finished to complement the house. The options you choose will affect how the porch will weather the outdoor elements, and they will help make it into a safe, comfortable haven for you and your family and friends to enjoy.

With the porch itself complete, consider how best to landscape around it and within it, from hanging baskets between columns to shrubs and flower beds along the base of the porch, adding color, texture, and a closeness to nature.

Finally, you'll add finishing touches to make your porch special and satisfy your personal tastes. Now's your chance; make the most of it.

◀◀ Even if an outdoor bathtub and all-glass shower aren't part of your plan, the details dedicated to this porch—and how they came to be—are no less impressive. The deep, copper-finished roof overhang, for instance, is enabled by an innovative roof framing system; the slatted railing system (set on top of a code-required solid wall) brings filtered light into the space. Potted plants provide natural color and texture against the concrete finishes.

► New construction affords you the flexibility to site the house and porch to optimize views, combat certain climate conditions, and provide multiple points of access. Here, a dramatic gable draws attention to the porch, putting it on equal footing with the house and interior spaces—an opportunity less likely in remodeling.

New Construction Advantages

✓ Design the house and porch together for a cohesive look and feel.

✓ Locate and design the porch to capture views, mitigate exposure to the elements, and direct traffic on and off the porch.

✓ Accommodate sloped areas or other site conditions within the over-all design of the house.

✓ Draw the eye to the porch or a primary area in the space (such as the front door).

✓ Arrange porch spaces so they are adjacent to interior rooms that work together and extend their use, providing multiple outdoor use areas.

✓ Use your lot, varying elevations, and multiple stories of the house to your maximum advantage.

✓ Consider a wider range of styles, materials, detailing, and finishes.

✓ Amortize and optimize costs as part of the overall project budget.

✓ Plan the porch for seasonal use and conversions that accommodate different climates.

NEW CONSTRUCTION

New construction allows you to start with a blank slate and only the conditions of your site and your imagination to guide you. It can be a dramatic process, with obvious progress occurring daily during the early stages of construction, then slowing down as the details are applied and finished.

Because there are so many decisions to make in new construction, it is critical to create a plan and stick with it, meeting deadlines along the way to maintain the building schedule and the budget.

A new construction project begins with a survey of the site to gauge existing conditions, limitations, and optimum use, including views, climate, and access. Next, you'll work with your design professional to determine a plan based on your lifestyle needs and what the site allows, including porches and outdoor areas and their connection to the house. Typically, your plans must go through an approvals process, in which they are reviewed for building code compliance and other regulatory standards, before construction can begin.

Approved plans in hand, your builder begins preparing the site, grading the soil to accommodate its foundation and providing underground access to the house for the homes plumbing, electrical and other systems. Within a few days, the floors and walls are framed—usually with wood, but perhaps with steel, concrete, or another structural system—after which a variety of trade contractors install electrical wiring, plumbing and mechanical systems, sewer drains and vents, insulation, windows and doors, and other products and systems hidden in or attached to the rough-framed structure. Sheathing and other weather barriers on the outside of the framing comprise the "envelope," while gypsum wallboard (or drywall) is installed on the interior walls, both acting as substrates for exterior and interior finishes, respectively.

At this point, the home's structure is three-dimensional, and it's easy to follow the original plans now as you walk through your house and it nears completion. Your porch areas have followed the same routine, leveraging the various trades and materials utilized for your home as an integral part of its design and construction.

Here's where the pace slows and a good relationship with your design professional and builder pays off as you become anxious at the apparent lack of progress. Rest assured; barring unexpected delays due to weather or material shortages, your builder is on track toward your agreed delivery date. That being said, it's never inappropriate to schedule time with your builder to ask questions, tour the house, and compare actual progress to the building schedule. A good builder welcomes the insight and inquiries of an educated home buyer, and is willing and able to guide you through the entire process, most critically as the project nears its end and you prepare to move in.

Any construction project can be somewhat arduous, but the result of your preparation and hard work is a place (and a porch) to call home.

The Convertible Porch

Whether you're building new or adding a porch to an existing home, you may want to consider the advantage of a multiseason porch. While most residential porches are open to the elements year-round, climate conditions may preclude or limit their use during certain seasons. If you have the opportunity to create a convertible porch, consider these tips:

✓ Select windows that allow you to swap out glass panes for screens, or add concealed tracks to install screen material over an opening.

✓ Choose materials and finishes, including furniture, that are tough enough to handle a variety of extreme climate conditions, or can be moved inside or out of harm's way when necessary.

✓ Consider outdoor heaters, a fireplace, or a woodstove to use during chilly evenings, no matter the season.

✓ Create sheltered outdoor alcoves to maintain small connections with the outside.

► Remodeling requires with existing conditions to match or complement forms, proportions, style, and materials. Adding or remodeling a porch boosts the design, function, and value of the house and enhances your quality of life.

Remodeling Advantages

✓ Retain your current location while increasing the value and enjoyment of your property.

✓ Preserves historic or period styles, materials, and details compatible with your residence.

✓ Increase the function of interior spaces with an added connection to the outside.

✓ Create and increase usable living space at a fraction of the cost of adding or remodeling an interior room, and with far less intrusion on your daily life.

✓ Improve your connection with nature and your neighborhood.

✓ Provide visitors with a comfortable and inviting transition from the outside to the inside.

✓ Enhance your home by adding to its uses and features.

✓ Add presence and depth to the front of your house while clearly identifying its main point of entry.

✓ Capture a previously neglected or underappreciated view.

REMODEL

Unlike new construction, adding or remodeling a porch requires a respect for and adherence to the existing conditions of your house, its lot, and your surrounding environment. Remodeling professionals enjoy the challenge of matching or complementing an architectural style and the look and feel of certain historic or period materials and finishes, and uncovering any mysteries they might contain. Every job presents a unique set of challenges, with the reward of enhancing the function and value of your home.

For the most part, homeowners remodel because they want to stay where they are and simply improve what they have. Porches and sunrooms, specifically, are popular projects for several reasons: They add instant value, both as a usable space and in terms of resale value; done well, they can turn a drab front entry into an inviting feature, provide greater access to multiple rooms inside the house, or expose a neglected view; and they generally require less time and money to complete compared to a room addition of the same size and scope, building a new home or moving.

Your design professional, ideally one skilled in residential remodeling, will take great care in making sure your new or remodeled porch suits your house and the character of your neighborhood while also addressing any specific lifestyle needs and desires.

As with new construction, most remodeling projects require approval by the local building authority prior to construction to ensure that the porch or sunroom complies with building codes and, in some cases, historic or community design guidelines followed in your particular area or neighborhood.

In many ways, your existing house or porch will dictate not just the design but also the materials and construction methods used to build or remodel the space.

Though generally following a similar process as the construction of a new house, a remodeled porch or sunroom includes a demolition and tie-in phase that may reveal new problems with the existing house or porch that need to be solved before proceeding, a situation more common with older homes and those remodeled previously.

Chances are good that you'll be able to maintain your daily routines while a porch or sunroom is being built or updated. Although there may be some inconveniences (such as having to use the back or side door while your contractor fashions a new front porch and entry door system), the payback is tremendous.

Rely on your design professional and builder to transform what you want and need in a new or remodeled porch or sunroom into a worthwhile space that goes even beyond your dreams. Once it's completed, you'll not only have an area to commune with your neighbors and with nature, but a special place to spend by yourself, with family and friends. And you may even inspire others to follow suit, improving the curb appeal and overall value of the entire neighborhood.

Adapting Existing Space

Just as porches can be converted to accommodate different seasons or climate conditions, so too can a space be altered not only to change its basic use, but also to create changing functionality to suit your needs. Consider these tips to adapting existing space:

✓ Transform a deck or open balcony into a covered porch or veranda to extend its seasonal use to spring, summer, and autumn.

✓ Use light and mobile furniture (including barbecue grills) that can be moved in and out of the porch to customize it and accommodate different gatherings or events.

✓ Design a supplemental artificial lighting scheme that alters the character and usability of the space, and include outlets for occasional floor and table lamps.

✓ Take advantage of a sloping hillside lot by using the underside of the new porch addition to store seasonal outdoor features and equipment.

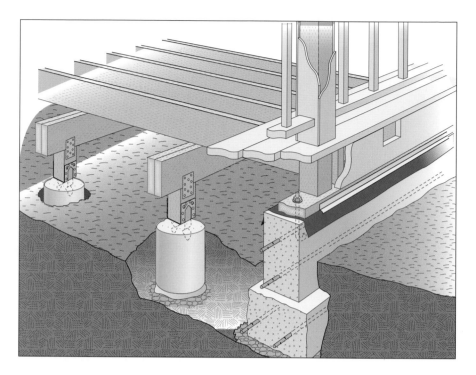

▲ Slab-on-grade (top), pier and beam (center), and perimeter wall (bottom) foundations.

THE FOUNDATION

The foundation is the first building block of your porch, anchoring it to the site, outlining its footprint, and providing structural support. Many foundation variations are reserved for special conditions, such as clay- or sand-rich soils, shallow frost lines, and steep slopes. Most common are the following foundation types:

Slab-on-Grade. A slab is flat-poured concrete over a perimeter footing system, reserved for at- or near-grade porches. It offers maximum durability and stability for the porch structure above, and require the least amount of labor and material costs per square foot of structural area compared to other foundations.

Pier and Beam. Also referred to as a "raised floor" foundation, this system relies on treated-wood piers on poured concrete footings set deep into the soil to connect to beams and floor joists, creating the basic structural frame for the porch. Generally used for sloped lots or porches higher than a few feet above grade, this foundation is engineered for the design and use of the porch and the anticipated weight it must carry. These foundations require provisions for air circulation to vent moisture away from the wood framing members.

Perimeter Wall. Like in a basement, concrete foundation walls extend above grade and include integral ledges on the inside face to accommodate beams and floor-frame members. The exposed concrete wall is sometimes faced with brick or stone.

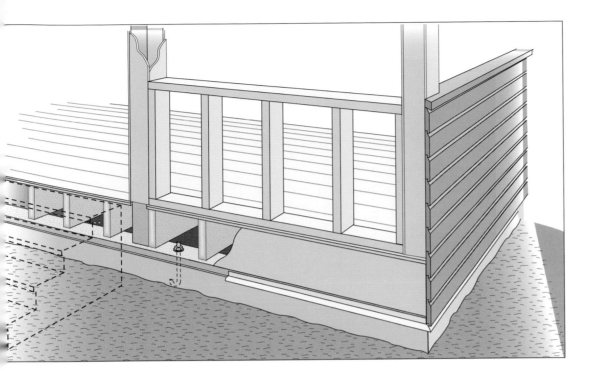

▼ Structural columns and other vertical framing members are attached securely to the concrete or wood-frame platform of the porch. They support horizontal railings and walls between them, as well as the roof overhang. Often, these vertical member extend below the deck plane to the foundation for added stability.

SUPPORT FRAMING

Support framing for a porch requires careful consideration of its features and elements, including the size and weight of the roof overhang, the span and materials of the railing, the integration of a permanent fireplace or similar feature, and lighting and other fixtures integral to the porch. All of these components combine to create a certain load, or weight, that will bear down on and be carried to the foundation by the support framing.

In addition to being engineered to adequately carry and share the load of the porch's various features, support members are integral to the foundation, bolted or embedded in place to ensure stability, and similarly attached to the roof framing and railing. Extra provisions may be required by code to accommodate seismic activity or extreme winds (such as for porches along the coast); various metal connectors supplement basic fasteners to provide additional stability and protection in extreme conditions and climates.

Support members are typically framed using solid or engineered wood; the latter affords the design of longer spans without sagging or bounce. For extremely long, open spans, perhaps to enable an unobstructed view from the porch, your builder or engineer may specify a steel beam across that span, which offers a shallower depth than a comparably engineered wood beam and can be concealed, or boxed, to make it compatible with the rest of the porch elements.

Structural supports complete the basic frame of your porch, providing a solid substrate for the rest of your porch's construction and finishes.

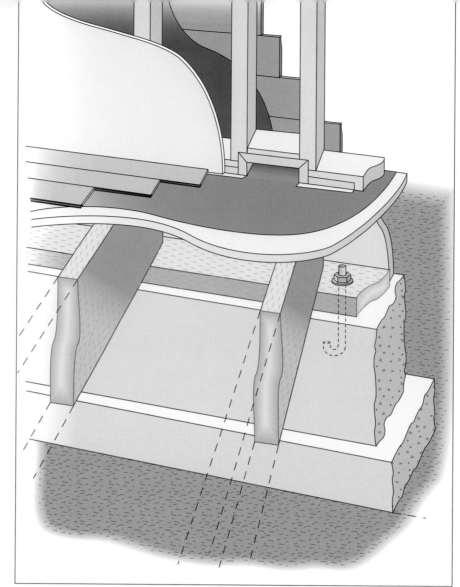

▲ Wood decking planks, as are shown here, are fastened directly to the floor frame. All other types of finished flooring, whether tile, stone, brick, carpet, or hardwood, attach to a structural subfloor with a waterproof membrane of building paper beneath it to protect the frame. Consult your design team to specify materials able to withstand the elements in your climate and the activities planned for the porch.

SUBFLOORS

On raised-floor foundations that will support a finished floor, a subfloor of exterior-grade, tongue-and-groove plywood or oriented strand board (OSB) panels, fastened with screws and glued to the floor joists, rests on the sill plate and piers. The subfloor stabilizes the floor frame structure. It also provides a flat platform and a solid substrate to which the porch's finished flooring materials will be attached. Slab foundations require no subfloor, though thin strips of wood (called sleepers) may be installed across a slab's surface to provide nailing points for attaching a wooden floor finish. For plank-wood floors, which superficially resemble the surface of a typical outdoor deck, the long wood planks require no subfloor and are nailed or screwed directly to the floor frame members. The application of the subfloor, the construction of the steps or stairs leading to the porch, and installation of the wall framing complete the rough construction of your porch, except for the roof.

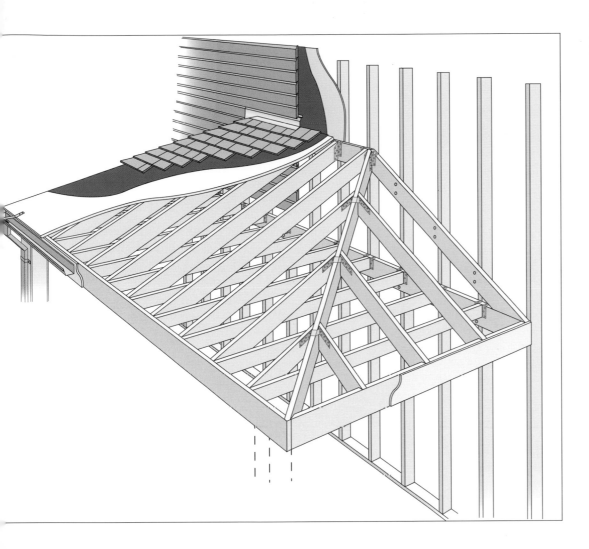

PORCH ROOFS

Most porch roofs are wood-framed, either as prebuilt trusses or as frame components built on the site. Attaching a roof to an existing house means removing the house's siding, stucco, or other finish material, opening the sheathing to the frame studs, and attaching a horizontal ledger board to the wall frame. The roof trusses are joined to this ledger board, either with nails or structural hangers. The roof frame receives a layer of exterior-grade plywood or OSB to stabilize the structure and provide a substrate for attaching the finished roofing material over a waterproof membrane of construction paper. Similarly, the underside of the roof frame may also be finished with a sheathing panel, providing a flat surface for a finished ceiling treatment such as tongue-and-groove planks, or left exposed for an open ceiling. The roof framing also supports lighting fixtures, electrical wiring, and insulation concealed by the finished ceiling.

▲ In addition to providing shelter over the porch, the roof frame is the substrate for finished roofing materials and sheds, or directs water away from, the front of the porch, either by design or in tandem with a gutter system.

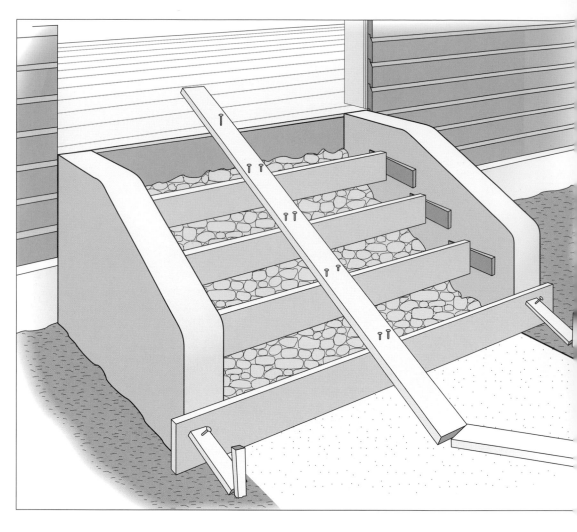

The placement, design, and materials of the steps or staircase help set a welcoming tone for the porch or indicate a more private space. Concrete steps can be infused with color (or pigmented) to soften their hue and complement or contrast the porch and house. Here, the steps replicate the color of the home's foundation walls, anchoring the second-story porch to its site.

STEPS AND STAIRCASES

Depending primarily on the style of the porch and the height it is raised above the grade, the steps or staircase leading to it may be either formed and poured with concrete or framed with wood. Though concrete typically provides a more durable and lasting structure, both are durable solutions. Practically, a choice between them is mostly aesthetic. Both types, however, require a high level of skill to plan and build.

Concrete steps are usually formed in a two-part process. First, side forms are built and concrete is poured for the two side walls that will support the handrails. When the side walls have cured, a second set of wooden forms is built between them to mold the horizontal steps (called treads) and vertical edges (or risers) of the finished stairs. These forms have steel reinforcement bars positioned inside them to strengthen the steps after the concrete hardens. For the second pour, workers fill the forms, allow the concrete to set up and

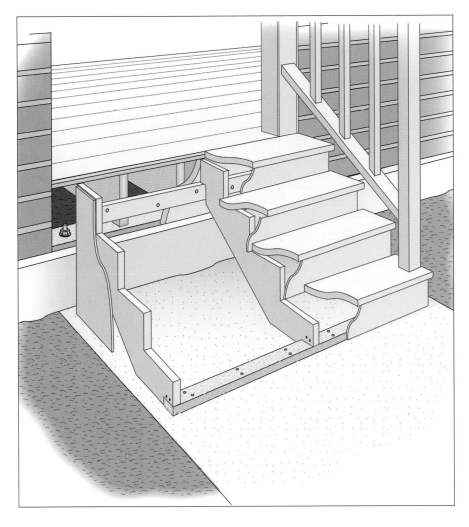

▼ Wood delivers a warmer approach to the porch than concrete but also typically requires more maintenance. Below, a solid half wall built as part of the stair's construction encloses the porch to comply with code requirements for safety, adds stability to the steps, and extends the porch's half-wall railing design down to the walk.

slip the vertical wood members out of the concrete. They fill the voids left by the forms, stamp patterns or screed and steel the surface until it is smooth, and embed any post connectors. The concrete is then allowed to set up completely. Within a day, the forms are stripped away. Several more days must pass before the concrete cures enough bear weight, continuing to cure for a month or more.

Wooden stairs and steps are constructed of structural lumber, usually pressure-treated to prevent fungal disease due to moisture. Built in place, their primary structural component is a pair or more of diagonal stringers with cutout notches for the steps. These stringers rest on and are attached at the top to the porch frame or foundation, and they extend from the porch to a concrete footing or ledger on the ground. In the same manner used for framing a floor or a porch deck, the treads and vertical risers span the stringers and are fastened to them. The stringers also are anchors for the king and newel posts that support the handrails and complete the stairs' structural frame.

▲ Porches can be served by a variety of utilities depending on their intended use, including plumbing for an outdoor kitchen and electrical wiring for lighting, security systems, intercoms, and audio speakers, among products that enhance the experience.

HOOKED UP

Porches today are increasingly multifunctional spaces, asked to serve family and friends throughout the day and evening hours and enable a variety of activities. As such, they require utilities to service those endeavors, a phase of construction traditionally reserved for indoor spaces.

Electricity is the most common utility service brought to the porch, relied upon primarily for lighting and outlets, and more recently to power security and entertainment systems, as well. Depending on the extent of the electrical demand (or load) planned for your porch, the service may require one or more dedicated circuits drawn from your house's main electrical panel or from a subpanel closer to the porch. Low-voltage wiring, which lessens the load, may be used for certain types of lighting. Pair it with other products such as fluorescent bulbs to help save energy.

Because your porch is a gateway to your home, security is a critical consideration. Motion sensors that trigger floodlights are a common solution, while more sophisticated closed-circuit video and voice systems offer a higher level of security—and often also serve as an effective communication system between the porch and the inside of the house.

Plumbing is also making its way onto the porch to serve the growing popularity of outdoor kitchens and bathrooms, including water systems for sinks, appliances, and drip irrigation systems and natural gas lines for cooking grills, lighting stands, and fireplaces. Raised-floor systems provide a way to conceal plumbing pipes and gas lines under the finished porch platform, stubbing up through the floor where necessary to serve various products and systems. Water service to a sink or appliance (such as a dishwasher or ice maker) requires you to provide a corresponding drain and wastewater connection, tied to the main house plumbing system.

Porches and sunrooms that are extensions of indoor space may also benefit from a heating and cooling system. Either extended from the home's main equipment or set up as a stand-alone design, the system regulates the climate and comfort of the porch or sunroom the same way it would an indoor room or area, including ventilation and humidity control should the climate demand it. Freezing climates require special considerations.

CEILINGS

Ceiling finish materials run the gamut, from tongue-and-groove wood planks similar to traditional finish-hardwood flooring to those that integrate a traditional beadboard texture (all of which can be varnished, painted, or stained), from reflective metal slats to decorative tin tiles, and from vaulted stucco in a Mediterranean-style porch to the exposed beams of a farmhouse.

Ceilings are an important part of your porch's design and finish, helping establish and nurture the intended experience. Most porches enclose the roof overhang with a flat (or "dropped") ceiling treatment, commonly a variation of wood planks, to maintain a comfortable scale, conceal electrical wiring and the housing for light fixtures, and as another surface on which to place an appropriate texture, color, or other detail that complements the porch's design.

On a front porch where the entrance to the house is the primary focus, the ceiling treatment of a gabled or vaulted roof design over the door will occasionally feature a different finish or treatment from the rest of the porch, such as a darker stain or paint to draw the eye down to the door or a different pattern or texture that reinforces the focus on the entry. Both dropped and vaulted ceilings require access into the space to repair and maintain the wiring and lighting equipment.

For more rustic porches—those that are intended to create an outdoor feel or experience—the roof structure may be left exposed or open to reveal the various framing components or finished in a vaulted ceiling. Such designs require careful installation of the roof overhang, and they may also need a veneer facing of finished planking material between the exposed roof rafters to conceal and finish the sheathing panel substrate of the roof's underside where it shows through the frame.

The materials used to finish a porch ceiling have evolved to meet the demand for low maintenance, faster and easier installation, and distinctive style. Once limited to wood or metal, and often in thin planks, ceiling systems are now available in larger panels (like plywood) and more durable materials, including composite woods, lightweight polymers, and various metals, such as copper and aluminum.

▲ Ceiling treatments reflect the style and character of a porch (above), providing either drama with an open, vaulted ceiling (seen on the second floor porch), or a traditional finished ceiling (first floor). Various ceiling treatments include natural strip plank (top left), painted tongue-and-groove planks (top center), and exposed framing (top right).

▲ Windows are a visual conduit from the inside of the house into and through the porch, providing a measure of security as well as framing views, shielding the weather and sunlight, and adding dimension to the porch.

WINDOWS

Occasionally, a porch design will include windows—as opposed to open frames or screened openings—to further protect the space and its contents (and you) from weather and pests. As a result, the porch delivers an experience more like an interior room than an outdoor area. Windows, whether on the house or as part of the porch, also reflect light coming into the porch (from the sun, porch fixtures, or inside the house) and frame views into and through the porch.

While window screens and blinds serve the practical purpose of keeping out excessive light and pesky pests while still allowing airflow into the house or porch, they also may limit the connection between the porch and the inside spaces.

Consider the operation of windows that look onto and through the porch; a fixed or picture window does not allow any ventilation or airflow between the spaces, but a casement (out-swing) window can affect the placement and proximity of the porch furniture to avoid the open sash. A single- or double-hung window, meanwhile, provides ventilation without intruding on the porch area. Windows can also be outfitted or built with integral grill patterns that replicate the existing windows of the house or a particular style you want to achieve.

TRIMWORK

While it certainly requires carpentry skills to frame a porch, build stairs, and install utilities and other features, true craftsmen look forward to the final phase of carpentry: the creation and application of the trim details. Finely detailed trimwork often commands attention, whether it's a subtle change in dimension or a dramatic design.

Trim details include the design of the railing's balustrade, the treatment around the door and window frames, the depth and dimension of the fascia, and the application of decorative features within the porch openings—all, of course, in keeping with the architectural style and character of your porch.

Trimwork is typically constructed of wood. Because moldings and trim are always in full view, trimwork requires the most meticulous application of any carpentry phase. Such materials are also among the most exposed components of a porch, often taking the brunt of the climate conditions. As such, they need to be finished with several coats of paint or stain and varnish (see page 165), and periodically refinished to maintain their good looks and structural integrity. Stone and steel components are more durable, but generally these materials offer fewer design choices than wood, especially for ornately finished porches and sunrooms.

▲ Trim details are the finishing touches to your porch or sunroom, providing more textural and dimensional layers and reinforcing the character of the design aspects of the porch. Take care to stay within the style and historical period of the porch and those of your house, since the right trim and other design details can easily enhance the aesthetic value of the space.

▲ With the structural work done, your porch is a blank slate awaiting a variety of finishing touches depending on its intended use, exposure to climate conditions, and your personal taste. Always protect the structural and finish elements of your porch properly to ensure lasting enjoyment and value.

COMPLETING THE PROJECT

Until now, your design and construction decisions have been driven primarily by factors beyond your control, such as the condition of your site, the prevailing style and materials of your home, and climate considerations, among others.

Now that the basic construction of your porch is done, however, you have some freedom to explore and apply your own taste as you choose finishing colors, fixtures, and furnishings for the porch. While remaining respectful of your porch's character and style, these finishing touches bring your individuality and creativity to the project.

In addition to making a style statement, those choices must also consider issues of upkeep and repair. Narrow your selections to finishes that suit your skill set and budget to properly maintain them, allowing you to not only enjoy your porch, but also preserve its value for years to come.

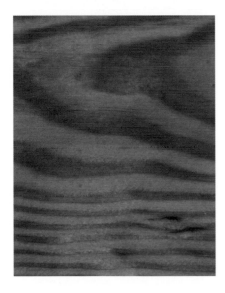

◀ A wide variety of stains and varnishes enhance and protect wood's natural beauty on ceilings, walls, floors, railings, and trimwork, allowing you to match or complement the finishes on your home. Oil finishes (upper left), specifically linseed and tung oils, penetrate the wood's fibers. Oil is easier to apply but offers less protection than a built-up polyurethane or varnish coat; however, simply wiping on more oil can often repair minor scratches. Varnishes (middle left) deliver a high level of protection that increases with additional layers. Spar varnish, which contains a higher level of oil, dries faster and is ideal for outdoor use. Polyurethane finishes are actually varnishes made with polyurethane resin to make the finish even more protective and durable. Bleached wood finishes (bottom left) soften the surface fibers of the wood, resulting in softer and lighter tones. Once such finishes dry completely, the bleached surface (and color) can be preserved with a clear varnish. Use only bleach specified for wood. Stain (upper right) is the most popular finish, allowing you alter the color and bring out the surface grain of the wood; pastel stains conceal the grain. Stains apply evenly to hardwoods and are easily preserved with a varnish coat. Technically, pickling wood (middle right) is a method, not a finish. Usually applied to new wood to make it look old, modern "pickling stains" are typically heavily pigmented white or off-white stains known as glazing stains, available in oil- or water-based formulations. Finally, wood can be painted (lower right), concealing the grain and enabling more dramatic colors. It's a good idea to prime raw wood before applying one or more finish coats, which require no additional protection but may need to be retouched every few years.

▲ Landscaping around your porch is an essential component of its overall character and attraction, softening lines, shielding intrusive views or concealing equipment or exposed structural elements, and adding color and texture to the overall aesthetic.

LANDSCAPING A PORCH

Although not technically part of the porch structure and direct fixtures or furnishings, landscaping plays an important role in finishing the project and enjoying your space. Landscape features, from shrubs and trees to flower beds and garden sculptures, help soften the lines of the porch, provide seasonal color, bring nature closer to the house, and direct the eye and access onto the porch.

Thick landscaping, specifically shrubs and bushy trees, can be an effective means of maintaining privacy for certain sections of the porch. Use them in place of a permanent railing or porch enclosure to block an unsightly view or exposed elements and equipment, such as concrete piers, heating and cooling equipment, or utility meters.

If you have a passion for herb, vegetable, or flower gardening, consider designing your porch with a dedicated set of steps and a path to connect it with your plot, or create framed views from inside your house and on your porch to enjoy your handiwork.

In addition to plants, trees, and flowers, landscaping also encompasses built structures and the so-called hardscapes (paths, irrigation and lighting systems, and decks or patios) that extend the usefulness of the porch beyond its sheltered borders.

A stone, brick, or poured-concrete path, for instance, guides visitors to your porch and shows how or where they access it from the street, sidewalk, or yard. Your choice of materials should complement those of the porch and your house, perhaps picking up on a detail or accent on the facade. If your foundation is clad in brick, face the paths in a similar brick pattern. Paths can also connect your porch to other outdoor features, such as a freestanding gazebo or shed, or perhaps a water feature, thus tying various outdoor elements together and inviting guests to linger in the garden.

Porches at or near grade can be designed and built to spill out or step down to a patio or framed wood deck, extending the space to an unprotected yet still connected outdoor area. If possible or in character with your porch, carry the flooring material outdoors to the patio or deck as a cohesive design element.

▲ Strategically placed landscaping can help interrupt and soften long expanses, such as porch railings, adding visual interest and color to an otherwise monotonous scene. Hanging plants along the eaves also break up the mass and can be served with an unobtrusive drip watering system concealed in the trimwork.

▲ Multiple seating areas, an outdoor wet bar, rich finishes and a cohesive color scheme create an inviting porch environment.

▼ Subtle yet effective lighting along stair treads provides a thoughtful measure of safety.

TODAY'S PORCH

Porches today serve a variety of lifestyle needs and desires even within a limited space. Manufacturers have developed an impressive range of outdoor-quality appliances and other fixtures and furnishings to outfit any whim and want, especially for entertaining. Consider the possibilities:

Outdoor kitchens. No longer just a kettle grill rolled onto the porch, today's outdoor kitchens are fully functional spaces, complete with counters and cabinet space, refrigerators, ice makers, wine storage, cooking appliances, and even dedicated ventilation systems to exhaust smoke and odors. Look for these spaces to evolve even more as porch design catches up with demand.

Fireplaces. Today's gas fireplaces are the perfect complement to modern porches, providing an outdoor hearth that adds comfort and vibrancy to the space without the expense, hassle, or smoke issues associated with wood-burning units.

Electronics. Flat-screen, high-definition televisions are all the rage outside, allowing folks to enjoy sports or movies in the pleasantness of a cool summer breeze or with the sun-

set as a backdrop. Under the shelter of a porch, these low-profile screens are easier to shield from the weather and are often built into a porch wall for additional protection and an incorporated look. Also note that wireless sound systems for outdoor applications can be placed anywhere in the yard or on the porch.

Your porch project is now complete—at least in your imagination. You've taken the opportunity to think about how porches and sunrooms enhance the quality of life, add value to a home and property, connect us with neighbors and nature, and serve a variety of whimsical and practical functions.

You've seen spectacular examples of porch design and been directed to the details that set them apart. Along the way, you've witnessed what is possible no matter the circumstances, regardless of the size of a house.

Finally, you've been granted a crash course in construction, following the process from foundation to finishes toward a greater understanding and respect for how a porch construction project comes together. That journey included an education in structural construction, finishes, furnishings, and landscaping—essential elements to finishing a porch and achieving full enjoyment of the space.

Now you're ready to tackle your own porch project, transforming your dreams and desires into reality. You have a vision, a view, and the inspiration. Your porch is waiting.

▲ Support posts integrated into the fireplace structure deliver a sculpted detail that's carried throughout the outdoor kitchen. Thick concrete countertops help balance the mass of stone.

▼ Compact appliances suit the scale of a porch while adding another attractive design detail.

Acknowledgments

Special thanks is given to every individual and organization that provided assistance and information during the creation of this book. Our gratitude is also extended to the architects, designers, builders, photographers, and home owners who shared their projects with our readers. The results demonstrate their exceptional creative arts and crafts.

Dolezal & Associates
Book Development Team

President:
Robert J. Dolezal

Managing Director/Project Manager:
Barbara K. Dolezal

Editor-in-Chief:
Victoria Irwin

Art Design:
Gary Hespenheide
Hespenheide Design, Newbury Park, CA

Writers:
Rich Binsacca
Robert Dolezal

Photographic Art Director: John Rickard

Illustrator:
Ron Hildebrand
Hildebrand Design, San Francisco, CA

Photo Researchers:
Rich Binsacca
John Rickard
Michael Snow

Photoshop Artist:
Jerry Bates

This book was produced for Collins Design by

Dolezal & Associates
2176 Crossroads Place
Livermore, CA 94550
(925) 373-3394
www.dolezalpublishing.com

Photo Credits

Jeffrey Allen
pp. 56–61
Courtesy of Bill McGuire at
Nantucket Architecture Group Ltd.

Wayne Austin
p. 134
Courtesy of Americana Inc.

Alex Beatty
pp. 122–123
Courtesy of Luna Design Group

© Edward Binkley, AIA
p. 99 (Top R & Bot R)
Courtesy of BSB Architects &
Planners Inc.

© Roger Brooks
www.rogerbrooks.ca
p. 132 (Top R)
Courtesy of Lamoureux Architect Inc.

Tim Buchman
Cover and pp. 94–97
Courtesy of Miller Architecture

William Cameron
p. 132 (Bot L), 164
Courtesy of Archadeck of North
Atlanta

**Copper Development
Association**
p. 5 (Bot), 43 (Top), 44 (Bot L & R),
148
Courtesy of Copper Development
Association

Douglas Dun
p. 5 (Top), 12, 28
Courtesy of BAR Architects Inc.

James Grote
p. 137 (Bot), 143 (R)
Courtesy of Cream City
Construction Inc.

© Greg Hadley Photography
p. 14 (Top L), 29 (Top)
Courtesy of Vogan Associates

© Eric Haesloop
p. 40 (Bot L), 41 (Bot R)
Courtesy of © Turnbull Griffin
Haesloop Architects

Lauren Harrison
p. 169
Courtesy of Eric Harrison Builders

Ray Houser
p. 14 (Top R)
Courtesy of Norman B. Yelin Architect

Proctor Jones Jr.
p. 41 (Top L & R)
Courtesy of © Turnbull Griffin
Haesloop Architects

© 2005 Jennifer Jordan
pp. 10–11
Courtesy of Steven B. Chambers
Architects

James Karlovec
p. 31
Courtesy of Karlovec & Co. Inc.

Brad Lamoureux
p. 16, 17 (Top), 25 (Bot)
Courtesy of Lamoureux Architect Inc.

Garrett Laws
p. 157 (Top)
Courtesy of The Copper and Slate
Company

Robert Lemermeyer
www.eye51.com
p. 6, 34–35
Courtesy of Sturgess Architecture

Loewen™
p. 43 (Bot), 44 (Top L)
Courtesy of Loewen™

Matthew D. Long
p. 24
Courtesy of Pilli Development

Christopher Lovi, Lovi Photo NYC
p. 15 (Bot)
Courtesy of W. Timothy Hess, AIA

Macrae–Gibson Architects
pp. 120–121
Courtesy of Macrae–Gibson
Architects

Andrew H. Mann
p. 5 (6th), 130
Courtesy of © Turnbull Griffin
Haesloop

Kevin Miller
kevinmillerphoto.com
p. 27, 54–55, 64–69, 145 (R), 158,
161(Bot)
Courtesy of Lamoureux Architect Inc.

Mathew Millman
p. 40 (Top L & R)
Courtesy of © Turnbull Griffin
Haesloop Architects

Peter Powles
www.powlesphoto.com.
p. 5 (3rd), 32
Courtesy of Lamoureux Architect Inc.

Rod Reilly
p. 36–39
Courtesy of Simonton Windows®

John Rickard
p. 15 (Top), 18–21, 25 (Top), 26,
29 (Bot), 46–47, 50–53, 72–91,
100–103, 106–107, 112–119,
135–136, 137 (Top), 140–142,
143 (L), 144, 145 (L & Mid),
146–147, 150, 152, 154–156, 157
(Mid & Bot), 159–160, 161 (Top L,
Top Mid, Top R), 162–163, 165–167,
168 (Bot), 170

W. Garrett Scholes
pp. 124–129
Courtesy of TMS Architects
Interior Design by Lois Walker Valeo,
Cloth Company Interiors

Anne Soulé
p. 98, 99 (Top L)
© Everett & Soulé, courtesy of BSB
Architects & Planners Inc.

**©1998 Southern Living Inc.
Reprinted with permission**
p. 30
Courtesy of Steven B. Chambers
Architects

**Through The Lens
Management Inc.**
14500 RR12, Suite 20
Wimberley, TX 78676
(512) 847-7506
www.ttlmgt.com

Paul Bardagjy
All courtesy of Through The
Lens Management Inc.
pp. 62–63, 92–93, 104–105,
133

© Leigh Christian
www.leighchristianphoto.com
p. 168 (Top)

Greg Hursley
All courtesy of Through The
Lens Management Inc.
p, 5 (2nd & 4th), 22, 70

Kai Y. Tong, AIA
p. 14 (Bot L)
Courtesy of Kai Y. Tong, AIA,
Hopkins & Porter Construction Inc.

Michael Walmsley
p. 2, 48–49
Courtesy of Curtis Gelotte Architects

James F. Wilson
www.jfwfoto.com
p. 5 (5th), 17 (Bot), 42, 45, 108,
110–111, 139

Contributors

Americana Inc.
2688 E. Ponce de Leon Ave.
Decatur, GA 30030
(404) 378-4597
www.shutterblinds.com
Photography by Wayne Austin, p. 134

Archadeck of North Atlanta
Old Alabama Rd. East, Suite 105
Roswell, GA 30076-2194
(770) 640-0310
www.archadeck.com
Design & Photography by William Cameron,
p. 132 (Bot L), 164

BAR Architects Inc.
543 Howard St.
San Francisco, CA 94105
(415) 293-5700
www.bararch.com
Photography by Douglas Dun, p. 5 (Top), 12, 28

Barbee Architects Inc.
2116 Hancock Dr.
Austin, TX 78756
(512) 323-2116
www.barbeeinc.com
Photography by Paul Bardagjy, pp. 92–93

BGK Architects
1508 West 5th St., Suite 200
Austin, TX 78703
(512) 476-7133
www.bgkarchitects.com
Photography by Greg Hursley, p. 5(4th), 70

**Bloodgood Sharp Buster Architects &
Planners Inc.**
1601 West Lakes Parkway, Suite 200
West Des Moines, IA 50266
(515) 273-3020
www.bsbdesign.com
Photography by © Edward Binkley, AIA, p. 99
(Top R & Bot R)
Photography by Anne Soulé, p. 98, 99 (Top L)
Photography by James F. Wilson, p. 139

Steven B. Chambers Architects
2108 Boll St.
Dallas, TX 75204
(214) 368-7293
www.chambersarchitects.com
Photography by © 2005 Jennifer Jordan,
pp. 10–11
Reprinted with Permission, © 1998 Southern
Living Inc., p. 30

The Copper and Slate Company
238A Calvary St.
Waltham, MA 02453
(781) 893-1916
www.hbuilders.net
Photography by Garrett Laws, p. 157 (Top)

Copper Development Association
260 Madison Ave.
New York, NY 10016
(212) 251-7200
www.copper.org
Photography by Copper Development
Association, p. 5 (Bot), 43 (Top), 44 (Bot L
& R), 148

Cream City Construction, Inc.
3112 W. Highland Blvd.
Milwaukee, WI 53208
(414) 774-7870
www.creamcityconstruction.com
Photography by James Grote, p. 137 (Bot),
143 (R)

**Food for Buildings Architects and
Designers**
Castorstraat 10
2516 AM, Den Haag, Holland (Netherlands)
31–70–3153030
pp. 42–45, 148

Curtis Gelotte Architects
150 Lake St., Suite 208
Kirkland, WA 98033-6461
(425) 828-3081
www.gelotte.com
Photography by Michael Walmsley, p. 2, 48–49

Eric Harrison Builders
2007 Leberman Ln.
Austin, TX 78703
(512) 480-8160
harrisonehb@aol.com
Photography by Lauren Harrison, p. 169

W. Timothy Hess, AIA
31 Adams Ave.
Groton, MA 01450
(978) 448-9963
tim@plattbuilders.com
Builder: Crescent Construction
Photography by Christopher Lovi, p. 15 (Bot)

Nic Holland Architecture
3605 Chalkstone Cv.
Austin, TX 78730-3700
(512) 422-5621
nholland@austin.rr.com
Photography by © Leigh Christian, p. 168 (Top)

Hopkins & Porter Construction
12944-C Travilah Rd., Suite 204
Potomac, MD 20854
(301) 840-9121
www.hopkinsandporter.com
Photography by Kai Y. Tong, AIA, p.14 (Bot L)

Karlovec & Co. Inc.
17619 Winslow Rd.
Shaker Heights, OH 44120
(216) 767-1887
www.karlovec.com
Photography by James Karlovec, p. 31

Willem Kymmell Architect
8925 Monte Verde Ln.
Oregon House, CA 95962
(530) 898-6221
wkymmell@succeed.net
pp. 42–45, 148

Lamoureux Architect Inc.
3392 Marine Dr.
West Vancouver, British Columbia, Canada
V7V 1M9
(604) 925-5170
www.lamoureuxarchitect.ca
Photography by © Roger Brooks, p. 132 (Top R)
Photography by Brad Lamoureux, p. 16, 17 (Top),
25 (Bot)
Photography by Kevin Miller, p. 5 (6th), 27,
54–55, 64–69, 130, 145 (R), 158, 161 (Bot)
Photography by Peter Powles, p. 5 (3rd), 32

Loewen™
77 Highway 52 West
Steinbach, Manitoba, Canada. R5G 1B2
(204) 326-6446
www.loewen.com
Photography by Loewen™, p. 43 (Bot), 44
(Top L)

Kathryn Lott, AIA
2216 North River Hills Rd. #A
Austin, TX 78733-2145
(512) 263-8778
Photography by Greg Hursley, p. 5 (2nd), 22

Luna Design Group
50 Salem St. Bldg. A
Lynnfield, MA 01940-2663
(781) 245-6508
www.lunadesign.com
Photography by Alex Beatty, pp. 122–123

Macrae–Gibson Architects
450 Seventh Ave., Suite 2406
New York, NY 10001
(212) 294-2940
www.m-ga.com
Photography by Macrae-Gibson Architects,
pp. 120–121

Miller Architecture
Tony F. Miller, AIA
360 North Caswell Rd., Suite 200
Charlotte, NC. 28204
(704) 377-8500
www.millerarchitecture.com
Photography by Tim Buchman,
Cover and pp. 94–97

Miró Rivera Architects
505 Powell St.
Austin, TX 78703
(512) 477 7016
www.mirorivera.com
Photography by Paul Bardagjy, pp. 62–63

Geoffrey Mouen Architects
950 Celebration Blvd., Suite G
Celebration, FL 34747
(321) 939-0470
www.gmarchitects.com
Photography by James F. Wilson, p. 5 (5th),
108, 111(Top & Bot)

Nantucket Architecture Group Ltd.
Bill M^{C}Guire
P.O. Box 1814
Nantucket, MA 02554
(508) 228-5631
www.nantucketarchitecture.com
Photography by Jeffrey Allen, pp. 56–61

Steve Olsen Construction
El Dorado Hills, CA 95762
(916) 966-7882
Photography by John Rickard, pp. 82–87

Overland Partners
5101 Broadway
San Antonio, TX 78209
(210) 829-7003
www.overlandpartners.com
Photography by Paul Bardagjy, pp. 104–105

Pacific Oak Development Inc.
Erik Pilegaard
(916) 425-5858
Photography by John Rickard, pp. 78–81

Pilli Development
510 Third St.
Annapolis, MD 21403
(410) 458-3045
www.pillidevelopment.com
Photography by Matthew D. Long, p. 24

Scheurer Architects
20411 SW Birch St., Suite 330
Newport Beach, CA 92660
(949) 752-4009
www.scheurerarchitects.com
Photography by James F. Wilson, p. 17 (Bot)

Simonton Windows®
5300 Briscoe Rd.
Parksburg, WV 26105-8125
(800) SIMONTON
www.simonton.com
Photography by Rod Reilly, pp. 36–39

William Simpson, AIA
128 Camino Pablo
Orinda, CA 94563
(925) 254-7651
www.orindaarchitect.com
Photography by John Rickard, pp. 72–77,
168 (Bot)

Studio for Civil Architecture
462 Broadway
New York, NY 10013
(212) 625-3336
www.thecivilstudio.com
Photography by James F. Wilson, p. 110, 111
(Top & Mid)

Sturgess Architecture
200, 724 11 Ave. SW
Calgary, Alberta T2R 0E4, Canada
(403) 263-5700
www.sturgessarchitecture.com
Photography by Robert Lemermeyer, p. 6,
34–35

TMS Architects
1 Cate St.
Portsmouth, NH 03801
(603) 436-4274
www.tms-architects.com
Interior design by Lois Walker Valeo/Cloth
Company Interiors
Photography by W. Garrett Scholes, pp. 124–129

Charles B. Travis Architects
710 W. 14th St., Suite A
Austin, TX
(512) 476-1007
www.charlestravis.com
Photography by Paul Bardagjy, p. 133

© Turnbull Griffin Haesloop Architects
817 Bancroft Way
Berkeley, CA 94710
(510) 841-0910
www.tgharchs.com.
Photography by © Eric Haesloop,
p. 40 (Bot L), 41 (Bot R)
Photography by Andrew H. Mann,
p. 5 (6th), 130
Photography by Mathew Millman,
p. 40 (Top L & R)
Photography by Proctor Jones Jr.,
p. 41 (Top L & R)

Vogan Associates
13004 Wilton Oaks Dr.
Silver Springs, MD 20906
(301) 929-2852
www.voganassociates.com
Photography by © Greg Hadley, p. 14 (Top L),
29 (Top)

West View Products Inc.
1350 SE Shelton St.
Dallas, OR 97338
(800) 203-7557
www.westviewproducts.com
Photography by John Rickard, pp. 46–47

Leslie Wilks Interior Designer
1320 Allyn Ave.
St. Helena, CA 94563
(707) 963-8328
Photography by John Rickard, pp. 88–91

Norman B. Yelin Architect
1517 34th Ave.
Seattle, WA 98122
(206) 323-2707
www.nbyarchitect.com
Photography by Ray Houser, p. 14 (Top R)

Resources

American Home Furnishings Alliance
High Point, NC
(336) 884-5000
www.afma4u.org

American Institute of Architects (AIA)
Washington, D.C.
800-AIA-3837 (242-3837)
www.aia.org

American Institute of Building Design
Stratford, Connecticut 06615
(800) 366-2423
www.aibd.org

American Lighting Association
Dallas, TX
(800) BRIGHT IDEAS (274-4484)
www.americanlightingassoc.com

American Society of Interior Designers
Washington, D.C.
(202) 546-3840
www.asid.org

Brick Industry Association
Reston, VA
(703) 620-0010
www.bia.org

Building Stone Institute
Itasca, Illinois
(630) 775-9130
www.buildingstone.org

Cedar Shake & Shingle Bureau
Sumas, WA
(604) 820-7700
www.cedarbureau.org

Composite Panel Association/Composite Wood Council
Gaithersburg, MD
(301) 670-0604
www.pbmdf.com

Copper Development Association
New York
(800) CDA-DATA (232-3282)
www.cda-copper.org

International Code Council
Falls Church, VA
(888) ICC-SAFE (422-7233)
www.iccsafe.org

International Concrete Repair Institute
Des Plaines, IL
(847) 827-0830
www.icri.org

International Wood Products Association
Alexandria, VA
(703) 820-6696
www.iwpawood.org

Metal Roofing Alliance
Belfair, WA
(360) 275-6161
www.metalroofing.com

National Association of Home Builders
(incl. Remodelors Council)
Washington, D.C.
(800) 368-5242
www.nahb.org

National Association of the Remodeling Industry
Des Plaines, IL
(847) 298-9200
www.remodeltoday.com

National Concrete Masonry Association
Herndon, VA
(703) 713-1900
www.ncma.org

National Paint and Coatings Association
Washington, D.C.
(202) 462-6267
www.paint.org

National Sunroom Association
Topeka, KS
(785) 271-0208
www.nationalsunroom.org

Portland Cement Association
Skokie, IL
(847) 966-6200
www.cement.org

Sealant, Waterproofing & Restoration Institute
Kansas City, MO
(816) 472-SWRI (472-7974)
www.swrionline.org

Southern Pine Council
Kenner, LA
(504) 443-4464
www.southernpine.com

Tile Council of North America
Anderson, SC
(864) 646-TILE (646-8453)
www.tileusa.com

Western Wood Products Association
Portland, OR
(503) 224-3930
www.wwpa.org

Window Coverings Association of America
Grover, MO 63040
(888) 298-9222
www.wcaa.org

Window Covering Manufacturers Association
New York, NY
(212) 297-2122
www.wcmanet.org

The Wood Flooring Manufacturers Association
Memphis, TN
(901) 526-5016
www.nofma.org

Wood Promotion Network
Chicago, IL
(866) 275-9663
www.beconstructive.com

Index

Index (continued)